C000193430

THE ROAD

TO MY

DAUGHTER

ELISABETH SPENCER

THE ROAD

TO MY

DAUGHTER

A MOTHER'S EXPERIENCE OF
THE TRANSGENDER JOURNEY

Biteback Publishing

ISBN 978-1-78590-649-7

10 9 8 7 6 5 4 3 2 1

A CIP catalogue record for this book is available from the British Library.

Set in Adobe Caslon Pro and Futura

Printed and bound in Great Britain by
CPI Group (UK) Ltd, Croydon CR0 4YY

PREFACE

Do I have a right to write this story? The road that trans people must travel to realise themselves fully, unfurling their truth before the world, is a long and painful one. Every step along that way is tangled with fear and provocation, and too often each moment of personal courage and joy is poisoned by the incomprehension and insensitivity of those around them.

As the mother of a trans daughter, I have walked that road with my child and I have, in some small part, suffered her pain. I fully understand that her suffering – and that of her countless trans siblings across the world and across time – is her own story to tell. I can only ever be an onlooker in this experience. But I too have my story. Loving a child with the fierce and unshakeable love that is born with an infant's first cry in a new world reaches inward to the spirit and beyond physical form.

That tiny person I gave birth to is still a part of me, and her journey will, in some way, always be mine.

When my daughter first came out as trans I was lost in a sea of ignorance. I knew nothing of the journey ahead. And so, when we finally arrived at the end of that road and my daughter was reborn in her true self, I wanted to write about my own journey from bewilderment to understanding.

In this memoir, when I talk about my daughter's childhood I have tried to reflect that time of confusion by using the male pronouns – until the point in my own story where my own eyes were opened. I am very aware that this is counter to the emotional and social narrative that she and all trans people carry with them, and no slur on trans identity is intended. I know that all my daughter's experiences of her young life were as a female child, and my choice of pronouns is intended to highlight the cruel burden of distress that I caused by my own ignorance at the time. These days I actually find it very difficult to remember when things were otherwise and navigating the pronouns in this way now feels very uncomfortable to me. A sign, I hope, of how far I have come.

This book is, in many ways, less a memoir than a meditation. I have tried to reflect upon aspects of science, medicine, history and psychology that have helped me understand where my daughter had to go and why. I hope that these brief detours might not only be useful to other parents of trans children (whatever age they might be) but that they might also add something to the public discussion, which is all too often tainted with false information. I have included such general background in response to the great fascination and endless questions I have encountered when talking to people about my own experience as a parent of a trans child.

Finally, this book was written with the support of my daughter. She is passionate about trans education and has graciously allowed me to share intimate details of her journey in the hope that it will help others. All names and places have been changed to protect my daughter's privacy. This includes the names of doctors and medical institutions: this is not a 'how to' handbook and anyone on their own path to transitioning should thoroughly research the medical care that is best for them.

This book is written with great humility and gratitude for the lessons I learnt on the road to my daughter.

PROLOGUE

I would love to start by saying I always knew. That she loved butterflies and unicorns, or had a penchant for pink. That questions had tugged at the edge of my mind when I saw her look longingly at the sparkly trainers and then turn away, or that she loved to play at dressing up and always chose to be the princess. It would be so much easier if I could say those things; but I can't. Not one of them ever happened. I simply had no idea. And so when the day came that my child, the young person whom I had only and always known as my son, decided there was no longer any choice but to say, 'There's something I need to tell you…', I was completely unprepared, in every way. A tsunami was about to change the landscape of both our lives for ever.

This book is the story of my journey through bewilderment, grief and fear to a conclusion that would have been unimaginable just a few years ago. It is a story of great courage (hers) and endless shortcomings (mine), of learning and growing, and of coming face to face with raw truths and inner demons that I didn't even know were there. My education has been profound. I have discovered things about the body and well-being that had never before been in my consciousness and I have come to learn of the deep suffering of people who, to me, if I thought about it at all, had only ever been marginal curiosities. I have seen my child experience vitriol, humiliation and prejudice, as well as huge generosity and care. I have seen my wider family fracture under the strain.

The journey has been both arduous and inspiring and has taught me as much about myself as it has about society, the nature of gender and sexuality and the body. It has also stretched me to the very edge of my emotional and psychological reserves. From its beginnings in Australia, through life in a small Cambridgeshire village, a famous college choir and an English public school, via the NHS, Harley Street, Belgium and Bangkok, this is the road I travelled.

I thought I had a son. I have a daughter.

CHAPTER 1

I was a reluctant mother, or at least I think not naturally
maternal. My own mother had always labelled me as
'the one least suited', but to that extent I was probably always a black sheep in her eyes. I had dreams and
aspirations beyond my circumstances in a middle-class
Australian home and, as it happened, as a young musician it was becoming apparent that I had the potential
to achieve those dreams too. While teachers talked of
university, my mother's ambitions for me rested no further than a clerical job in the bank or perhaps a comfortable secretarial position. I felt like a fish out of water
at home; angry, stifled and implacably determined to
escape to wider horizons. In 1980s Australia, at least in
my world, that meant England, and my sights were set
firmly on studying at music college in London. How I
navigated those teenage dreams and in time achieved
that goal is of little matter here, except for the quirk

of fate which meant that my determination found me in due course at the Royal Academy of Music, where my professor was the great flute player Gareth Morris. Renowned for his anecdotal style of teaching, in between scales and repertoire Morris's stories ranged from Dickens and horology to the importance of Pimm's on a summer's day. It was during one of these always stimulating chats that he told me about his sibling, the author Jan Morris, who started life as James and emerged from surgery in Morocco in a body reborn female. Transgenderism. I had never heard of such a possibility and could barely imagine either the path or the motivation that might lead someone to such a drastic and brutal choice. Always curious, I sought out Jan Morris's autobiographical account of her transgender journey, the extraordinary *Conundrum*, to learn more about this enigmatic condition, then put it on the shelf for thirty years while I got back to my flute.

Life, of course, went by. I married young and foolishly (and, as the adage would have it, repented at leisure). He was considerably older than me, sophisticated and intelligent with movie-star looks and from a cultural background that fascinated me, coming as I did from a social milieu that was, to say the least, lacking in diversity. Once we were married, though, it didn't take long for things to unravel. I remember clearly the first time his chilling anger found its outlet. I was a few minutes late to meet him from the train and he didn't even wait for a private moment. Pushing me violently against the car, he gripped my arm until it hurt, restraining me so that I couldn't edge away as he glared into my eyes. 'From now on you'll be here when I say.' He justified his actions, then and in the future, in the name of traditional values. I was there to serve him and that I would do. Once the demon was out of the box, it seemed there was no going back and I walked on eggshells and lived with a constant and sickening feeling of fear. The sound of his key in the door made my heart beat faster with unnameable anxiety. When I came home from work, the walk from the station was filled with a sense of mounting dread. I never knew what I would meet when I returned. Would I be simply ignored (those were good days) or would I be sworn at? Perhaps the washing was not done to his liking. Maybe he had run out of cigarettes or whisky. Would dinner be satisfactory today or would the plate be hurled at the wall so I had to clean the mess from the floor while he stood over me? Other torments were simply amusements to him. I would try to avoid him when he had a shower because I hated it when he whipped me with his towel, though apparently in his boarding school days this was quite the game and I should find it amusing too. Nothing I did was right, but I didn't know how to escape. I was eighteen when I married him.

Someone said to me not long ago that I always refer to this man from my past simply as 'my first husband'.

That is because I now have the power to render him opaque and nameless. The day my daughter eventually came out to him he repudiated her and turned his face away. And so, as he tried then to take away her identity, I have not given him one here. He did, however, have a role in bringing my two children into the world, and a role in their lives; the bearer of scars, and the creator of them. As a father, his part in this story cannot be erased, and it is true that in his final days, which came unexpectedly and too soon, he reached out in regret and sorrow. His heartfelt apology to my daughter was his dying gift to her, and there was redemption in his parting.

When, back in those desperate early days of marriage, I fell pregnant, I knew something had to change. With no family support in England, the best solution to the intractable dilemma of managing a baby and a career in music, which is defined by its irregular hours, late nights and unreliable income, seemed to be to return to Australia. I was not happy with this choice – having graduated, I was just beginning to find my feet in the London music scene – but at least I knew that my family would welcome me home as the prodigal daughter. And I suppose this is where the journey really begins.

Two years after that heart-wrenching move back to Australia, and still with my first husband, I was pregnant again. When I was carrying my first child, Lucas,

I had been unshakeably certain he was a boy from the first weeks of pregnancy. This time, the same intuition told me my baby was a girl. Lydia, I imagined, or perhaps Helena. I would talk to her and in my mind she replied, and the first foundations of our imagined relationship were laid. Hormones can do strange things to us. At the twenty-week scan the ultrasound technician asked the usual question. Would I like to know the sex? It seemed unnecessary to me, of course, as I felt in the core of my being that it was a girl, but it was expected and so I said yes. 'Well,' he said, 'this is an exciting moment ... and look, there we can see the third leg!' What? My baby had three legs? This was appalling news, and yet the technician seemed quite unfazed as he swiped the ultrasound device around my swollen belly. 'Look closely. Can you see it?' And then I realised; this feeble banter was his trademark medical joke. He was telling me my baby was a boy. I felt dizzy and disorientated. 'It's a boy?' I asked. 'You must be wrong. Absolutely not. I know you're wrong. It's definitely a girl.' But of course, the evidence was on the screen; I left the room in a daze.

I had no particular longing for a girl. I wasn't trying to create a pigeon pair with Lucas so I could congratulate myself on having achieved the ideal family unit and consider it a job well done. I was simply shaken to the core that my intuition had failed so drastically. I became disconnected and distanced from this coming baby, whom I now felt I didn't know at all. A visit to the park with two-year-old Lucas a few days later pulled me up sharply, though, when I watched another mother shining with love as she played with her child, a beautiful little boy with profound special needs. In a hot flush of shame, I recognised my self-indulgence and ridiculous notions for what they were. I should be looking forward to the birth of my child. A brother for Lucas. Oh yes, what fun we'd have together – my boys and I. Henry? Julius? Miles? My mental clock was reset and I decided to make a new beginning. Without a moment's thought to notions of gender fluidity, and unquestioning of more traditional norms, I began to count the blessings of being able to hand down clothes and toys, of only having to drive to cricket on Saturdays without factoring in the logistics of ballet lessons as well. As I said, hormones can do strange things to us.

And so, Miles was born, beautiful, healthy and enormous. I was rather proud of delivering a 10lb 4oz baby naturally and in a lightning-fast labour. My clearest memory of the event, though, was that in the haze of the excruciating pain I sank my teeth into my husband's arm. I bit him hard and wasn't sorry. His ways had not been reformed, and with that admittedly deplorable act I enjoyed a brief moment of ascendency. In a rather more rational line of thought, I also found relief in shouting, 'I am never, ever doing this again' (and I didn't). But, like most mothers, I loved that baby from its first breath and knew with absolute clarity that I would do anything to help him be the best and happiest that he could possibly be, to flourish in life, surrounded by love and opportunities.

I suppose that is every parent's hope and intention, but like every parent naturally I failed, and sometimes spectacularly, along the way. The newborn days were a nightmare. For the first forty-eight hours Miles slept like an angel, tightly swaddled in his baby blanket, as rounded and serene as a cherub. He fed well and was admired by everyone. Obviously, he was the most beautiful infant in the world, possibly ever. Until suddenly, he woke up. On day three, Miles started to scream relentlessly and for two whole years it felt like he would never stop. Up and down and up and down I walked him, through hallways and darkened rooms, around parks and shops, in buggies and slings, begging him to stop crying. Feeding was painful and sometimes the only answer was to put him in the car and drive endlessly around the back streets through the dark of the night. When he wasn't crying he was feeding, and my life contracted to a small circle of despair. Without my mother I think we might both have come to an early end; however, she stepped in selflessly, taking care of Lucas and Miles so I could go back to work, which was the only place I could be myself again. Now, as I look back on this time, I do sometimes wonder whether that newly born human being understood that its spirit had been made manifest in the wrong body and that the constant crying was a hopeless outpouring of despair at the situation. Was there somehow already an urgent desire to escape the erroneous body and put things right in this new physical dimension? We reflect on many things with hindsight, of course, and I recognise this is likely merely a flight of fancy, but, nonetheless, the memory of those days combined with my own unshakeable pregnant intuition makes the possibility seem not entirely far-fetched.

The early years went by in similar fashion. My mother was more like a second mother than a grandmother to my children as I juggled the responsibilities of working and providing for them (their father offering little in the way of such contribution). Lucas was by now in pre-school and Miles was a toddler. Every time I dropped Miles off at my mother's before work, my heart was wrenched as he hammered his tiny hands at the front window, crying 'Mummy, Mummy' as I walked away. I loved this child but felt that nothing I did ever brought him ease or comfort. He was very bright and so, of course, lively and interested in the world, but the poignant despair that I heard in his voice, even though Grandma's house was essentially his second home, never really seemed to leave him. From the earliest age there was a deep unhappiness in Miles that I could not fathom. I was aware of it and utterly blamed myself – for bringing a child into a toxic relationship in which

I felt inextricably entangled, for working too much or for closing the door to practise the flute, for lacking a genuine enthusiasm for Play-Doh, for being away with work or really just for anything I could think of.

Things settled down over time, as they generally do, and Miles developed his own fascinations and obsessions, usually involving the careful cataloguing of collections and a great desire for orderliness. Thomas the Tank Engine (and friends) littered the floor and lived in a little Thomas backpack. They were lined up daily for roll call and inspection. Micro Machines spread across the kitchen floor, engaged in ever more epic battles. There was endless rewinding of *Thunderbirds* videos and, now I think about it, a striking preference for Lady Penelope. I am now embarrassed by my outrageously gendered assumptions but, to me, then, Miles was the most boyish of little boys.

Perhaps when Miles started pre-school, had I been more alert, more present, or had any real awareness of concepts of gender fluidity, I might have started to see the first clues. I regret that I didn't but, in my defence, transgenderism was so far off my radar just twenty years ago I think it is unlikely I would even then have guessed what might lie beneath. In any case, I was sufficiently liberal in my thinking that I wasn't at all concerned by the pre-school teacher's report which said that Miles's favourite activity was playing in the doll corner. I did notice that most of his friends appeared to be girls and was touched by his inseparable friendship with one in particular, a delightful child named Lucy. But all properly brought up four-year-olds should, I thought, be able to play easily with both sexes. I took it, I suppose, as a mark of good socialisation and a small tick in the parenting box for me. Miles never showed any interest in wearing anything other than the standard issue boys' T-shirts and shorts (usually embellished with Thomas or Buzz Lightyear, depending on current preference), though I wonder if this might have been different if he had had a sister or girl cousins around to emulate. He did, however, have very strong feelings about his hair and constantly implored me not to have it cut but to let it grow long. On one occasion he cut a huge triangle out of his adorable fringe when no one was looking, and it is only recently that I learnt that my daughter clearly remembers doing this. Her childish thought process at the time was apparently that if she took drastic action, I would realise how much she wanted to be in charge of her own hair. Sadly, in this I let her down and responded instead as I think most mothers would, with a scolding and an emergency visit to the hairdresser.

Not long after the Great Hair Massacre, life veered wildly again when I was offered an opportunity I knew I couldn't refuse back in England, the country that still in many ways I called home. For the past three years, with the help of my mother, I'd found relief from the guilt and unremitting strain of Miles's constant despair by moonlighting as a university student. And it was there, in the mock-Oxbridge cloisters of the University of Western Australia's arts faculty, that I finally found myself. There I was liberated by literature and history, whirled around by post-modernism, shaken loose by feminist historiography and was eventually cast up on the mysterious shore of semiotics and hermeneutics. The hidden meaning of the text engrossed me, becoming a cipher for the confusion that had wracked my own life, and my unexpected success in this game of academia started to open up a new vision of my future. I realised now not just that I had the inner strength to escape my desperate marriage but that if I was to survive and grow, to reach my potential, I *had* to. There could be no compromise. UWA had given me the key to the door: a scholarship to Cambridge, higher studies, an undreamt-of new beginning.

I knew accepting this offer had the potential to change the entire course of my life and my children's future, and so, with a single-minded focus which hid my deep anxieties, I decided to take that leap into the dark. I would return to Europe along with Lucas, Miles and (for the time being) my husband. I agonised about leaving my mother, sister, brother and sister-in-law behind. They had provided stability and care for my children when often I felt incapable of it and withdrew into work as my retreat. I had largely survived these past few years as I juggled work and study thanks to their care and constant help, and I knew that without this practical and emotional support in England I would become vulnerable again in my disastrous marriage.

Over the years, I had left my husband on several occasions but each time succumbed to his promises of change and repentance and to his manipulative threats. I felt so guilty. But my most recent escape was sticking. I knew I could not let my children spend any more years thinking that this barrage of emotional and physical abuse was an acceptable way to treat a woman. It was too late to cover their ears from the words and their eyes from the sight of my fear, but I had reached a turning point. I had moved back to my mother's house with the two children, and she took care of them while I worked and studied. Now all of this had to change. Thanks to the Hague Convention on the Civil Aspects of International Child Abduction, my solicitor advised me that if I took the children out of the country without my husband's consent (and I knew he would never consent), I would have no chance of succeeding in keeping them in England. So, accepting one last time his promises to change and make a new start, I finally decided to take a chance on reconciliation and bring our family together again under one roof. I knew it would be difficult, but I hoped that with the opportunities it offered us we might not just survive but benefit. And so, with two small boys, one with a miniature violin and a stuffed fox under his arm, the other in a blue plastic raincoat ('It's my exoskeleton, Mummy, I'm a Ninja Turtle') and carrying a Thomas the Tank Engine back-pack full of trains, we walked, without looking back, through the airport security gates to start our life again.

CHAPTER 2

Writing about these early years and experiences, and in the same paragraph about my daughter's own recollections, I realise that I have slipped swiftly into the muddy vortex of gender pronouns and carelessly trampled on expectations of their use. For this I apologise; I am very aware of the importance of gender pronouns to the trans community and I have seen firsthand the pain and distress that misgendering can cause. The whole area is a complex and troubled one, and it leads quickly into discussion of what it means to be cisgendered or trans, the pitfalls of misgendering and the experimental world of gender-neutral pronouns. How people prefer to be referred to is as varied as the individuals themselves, and I have thought at length about how to approach the issue in writing this story. I know that my daughter experiences the whole narrative of her life as female and that, from her point of view, she was just as much a 'she' in those pre-school years as she is now. In our daily conversation, I try hard to remember this when we talk about the past together, though I still occasionally slip (and she will accept my apology, sometimes graciously, sometimes not). In telling of my own steps on the road that we have travelled together, I have decided, however, that I can only really shine light on that journey through the lens of my own experience.

For most of my daughter's life I, not unreasonably, believed her to be male. When I think of that three-year-old Thunderbirds enthusiast, Thomas and friends lined up for inspection on the kitchen floor and Buzz Lightyear heading to infinity and beyond, I see in my mind's eye a little boy, and to express that time in my life with any words other than 'he' or 'him' does not align with those memories. This does not mean that I discount or disrespect my daughter's absolute certainty of her innate early femininity, merely that I am telling this story as I lived it and not as she lived it. And so, the approach that I have decided on – and I do this in part to call out now my own failure to 'see' then – is that I will use male gender pronouns in writing about the years when I personally interacted with my child as the mother of a boy, but that I will use female gender pronouns when I write about my daughter from the point at which I began to properly recognise her as female, and when I recount her own recollections of earlier years.

The same applies to referring to my daughter through those years by the name of Miles. In this I am guilty of 'deadnaming', and I know this is as heinous and hurtful an error as using the wrong pronoun. Deadnaming is the act of referring to a trans person by their birth name rather than their chosen, affirmed name. It can happen accidentally and bureaucratically, for example, if documents are not updated; it can happen by carelessness or absent-mindedness in those who have a long association with the person (unfortunate, but usually just a question of habit which will adjust over time); but, worst of all, it can be done deliberately and cruelly, and often is. Family members and formerly close friends who refuse to accept the change may insist on using the name they have always known, and in this case it is nothing less than a hostile act of invalidation and an assault on the trans person's identity. I know that deadnaming is very painful and common and so, again, I apologise, but my reasoning is the same as I have applied to my use of gender pronouns (and it changes over the course of this story in the same way). In fact, Miles adopted a nickname from around the age of seven and became known as Milly to everyone outside the family. At that time she begged me repeatedly to call her Milly, but I was shamefully slow to adopt her new chosen name and initially brushed it aside as a passing quirk. I liked the name Miles – I thought it was a strong and serious name and reflected, I suppose, something of what I hoped my child might become. Miles was, in short, the name that I had lovingly selected, and I was resistant to Milly's pleas. It has taken me a long time even to start to unpick the careless cruelty of so many of my actions, and I am ashamed and saddened now to think how thoughtlessly and selfishly I refused such a simple, life-defining request.

It was fifteen years until I understood that Milly had adopted her new name as a kind of gender-neutral halfway house. Feeling unable to come out publicly, by choosing a non-specific name she was at least able to shelter herself psychologically from the inescapable masculinity of the name Miles. Milly told me not long ago that the idea was actually inspired by her primary school French teacher, who recognised his pupil's immense anxiety at having to announce to the class 'je m'appelle...' Taking Milly aside after the lesson, he talked to her and helped her find a way around the problem, offering her the glimpse of a tiny haven. These days she is always Milly to me. I like it and I have boundless gratitude to that teacher who guided her towards one simple compromise that helped her survive. But most of all, I ache for that seven-year-old child who had to reach so deep just to navigate something we so easily take for granted. A name. An identity.

Under the general heading of 'things I have learnt' when it comes to trans identity and not hurting friends and loved ones, foremost among them is the importance of getting the gender pronouns right. For me, a useful rule of thumb has been to assume that the way a person currently presents in terms of gender indicates the pronoun you should use – both in the now and in talking about the past. Simpler still, just ask. Organisations that encourage their members to make known their preferred pronouns are not engaging in some kind of right-on virtue signalling, to be laughed at and avoided by those of us lucky enough not to wrestle with appearances on a daily basis; they are, in fact, showing a small respect that recognises the potential for deep complexity in matters of gender identity. What little does it cost us to respond in turn with that same respect? As I have learnt, not all trans people will necessarily be at the stage of their journey where they outwardly present in their new physical, aesthetic or even behavioural identity. Nonetheless, they may (or will) be at that stage internally. Certainly, Milly went through this early in her process of transitioning before she was publicly 'out', but because I knew her well at least I knew her preferences and tried to understand and respect that need. It is, though, far more problematic from the outside, and I remember this period as one of the most painful times that had to be navigated. To me, it was understandable if people around us, even family members (and especially elderly ones), made mistakes. Milly felt otherwise, and there was a great deal of anger and many tears as she dealt with the sense of loss of identity and perceived insult that misgendering caused her. In response, she directed some of that outrage at me, feeling that I should be equally irate on her behalf. I know I did not stand up for her as I should have. Travelling the journey doesn't necessarily give you all the answers.

We arrived in Cambridge in September, before the house that had been allocated to me by my new college was available. It is hard to believe now, but in those days we had barely encountered the internet. Finding short-term accommodation and information about schools had required letters and phone calls from Australia, and I really had little idea of what lay ahead. I had found a hostel that could accommodate us for a few weeks but was looking forward to finally being able to settle into a home and routine again. The past months – selling the house, packing and shipping all our possessions, leaving jobs and colleagues, reaching an agreement with my husband, and most of all saying goodbye to family – had been incredibly stressful. I knew I was taking a giant leap in the dark but was worried I was throwing my children into the abyss with me. While Lucas was captivated by every element of his strange new home, Miles was withdrawn and miserable. He seemed worryingly disengaged and I supposed that he was missing everything that had been familiar. Looking back, I recognise it now as the first sign of the depression that defined and overwhelmed his childhood and adolescence. As usual, when it came to Miles I was haunted by guilt.

The reconciliation with my husband was not going well. Just a few weeks into the new arrangement, life returned to the way it always had been. I wasn't surprised. The shouting and drinking, the laziness and refusal to even countenance working. One of my first outings was a secret visit to a high street solicitor. How long would I need to live in England before it could be deemed my children's place of habitual residence? I needed the Hague Convention to swing in my favour by proving that the children were in a 'settled environment' before I could leave him again and, taking the long view, I was determined to tough it out. In the meantime, my primary aim was somehow to protect the children as much as I could from this toxic home life. How, I was not sure.

The first task was to find a suitable school for the boys. As a musician, I hoped that my children would share my love of music and be enriched by it, though I had no intention of pushing them into my world (in fact, I rather hoped their professional destiny might be in a somewhat more secure and better remunerated sphere). Nonetheless, Lucas was already showing promise, playing the piano with flair and experimenting with composing, and Miles was always singing and was starting to play the violin by ear. It seemed to be in the genes, and when it came to a musical education Cambridge was the perfect place. An ancient university city with several famed choral foundations, I thought life as a chorister in a choir school would offer the opportunities I wanted for Lucas and Miles – a sound, traditional education and a musical environment that was second to none. Miles was too young yet, but Lucas was the ideal age, having just turned eight. The voice trials (an audition process for choristers) were open to eight- and nine-year-old boys and they were coming up in a few weeks' time. I didn't realise then that aspiring choir mothers spent months training up their musical offspring and dragging them from one cathedral to the next to sing for organists far and wide. Instead, I found an old piano in the hostel, quickly taught Lucas the hymn 'Praise, my soul, the King of heaven' and to sing notes in a chord and made an application. I liked what I saw of the first choir school I visited, until the moment my tour took me to the school hall, where senior boys were in rehearsal for their end-of-term play. Thirteen-year-olds were running around dressed as fairies and damsels, wearing makeup, sparkly wings and long-haired wigs. My Australian sensibilities, still firmly rooted in traditional expectations of gender, were astounded; the chances of seeing such a sight in any Australian school were very slight and, to be very honest, I wasn't comfortable with it. The irony, of course, does not escape me.

And so I applied to the other school, its soaring gothic chapel home to one of the finest choirs in the country. Its choir is composed of sixteen boys and four

probationers, choristers who spend two years in training, shadowing the ones who have 'gone up' before
them. The school also provided an unexpected solution
to the problem of shielding my children from their
damaging family life. To accommodate their rigorous
schedule of morning and evening rehearsals, services,
instrumental practice and, of course, the school day, the
choristers have to board. I had never before considered
the option of boarding and, in fact, thought it was a
dreadful thing to do to a child of any age, let alone ones
so young. It was certainly very far from my own school
experience. Nonetheless, there was an equation to be
balanced, and boarding seemed like the lesser of two
evils. If Lucas (and later Miles) were admitted to the
choir, I thought it would give them protection, stability
and an exceptional cultural and musical experience, as
well as a private school education, which I could not
otherwise afford. So Lucas did the voice trial, sang his
hymn, played a tune, identified some intervals and the
die was cast. He became a boarding chorister, and Miles
went into pre-prep as a day boy at the same school.

I reconciled myself to the horrible idea of sending my
child to boarding school by living close enough to the
college that I could go to hear the choir sing every day.
I went to Evensong as often as I possibly could, often
several times a week, and on Sunday to Eucharist and
sometimes even to Matins as well. In between afternoon
rehearsal and Evensong, I would help with the choir

teas in the cloister rooms, simply because it was another opportunity to have a few minutes with Lucas and to give him a hug when no one was looking. After the service, parents would walk back to the boarding house and stand at the bottom of the stairs talking to the boys before they went into supper. And on Saturday and Sunday afternoons we were allowed to take them out for a few precious hours. The life of a boarding chorister is a rich but unnatural one. It was, though, or at least I thought it was, achieving the ends I had hoped for, and so when Miles was eight it was his turn for the voice trial. 'Praise, my soul, the King of heaven' was dusted off again and sung angelically, and all the necessary musical hoops were successfully jumped through. In fact, Miles surprised us all in the audition when it was discovered that he had perfect pitch – a rare ability to name any note upon hearing it either on its own or in a chord. The organist made a game of playing ever more complex harmonies to see how far he could go, but Miles was unstoppable. Everyone was rather convinced he would make an exceptional chorister.

* * *

Miles was the world's worst chorister.

From the day he became a probationer he hated every moment. He became ever more withdrawn and unhappy, never weeping with homesickness but appearing

emotionally disconnected. When he sang, his reluc-
tance was obvious; his eyes were always downcast and
he barely enunciated the words. As I walked with him
on his weekend exeats, he would drag his feet along the
riverside meadows muttering, 'I hate this country, I hate
it here. It's so cold, it's always grey. The food is terrible.
Why are we here, why am I here?' and so on and on
until it was time to go back for the afternoon rehearsal.
Of course, it wasn't always like that, but I knew there
was a constant sadness around him, and even though
the choir was so small that it was almost like a family,
he seemed isolated within it. Yet again I failed to spot
the warning signs of depression or any indication that
Miles was anything other than a homesick young
boarder, and because things had only become worse
at home I did everything I could to encourage him to
stick with it. Or, more honestly, I refused to allow him
to leave. I thought my bird's-eye view as an adult and a
mother meant that I could see advantages he couldn't,
that things would improve and that the choir offered
the best possible grounding for his evident and unusual
musical abilities. In later years, Milly and I have talked
about this a great deal and, surprisingly, these days she
agrees with me, if only to the extent that she acknowl-
edges the value of the intense musical grounding she
had there and its influence on her development as a
musician. But I do know now how damaging she found
it in so many other ways and I greatly regret my lack of

sensitivity to the depth of her suffering at the time and to the reasons for it. Ignorance is my only defence.

By the time Miles had been a full chorister for two years, life had changed dramatically. I had finally claimed the UK as the settled home of my children and left my husband. Lucas had moved on from choir school and was now a music scholar at a leading boys' public school, and Miles had stopped muttering 'I hate it here' (though self-evidently he still did). It was during this time that Miles discovered there was a world of music beyond canticles and anthems and the piano, all of which he loathed. First, he asked if I would let him play my old flute. I started to teach him and he took to it immediately. Suddenly he seemed more comfortable, and his musical engine, which had completely stalled in the choir, was reignited. Milly told me much later that it was because to her, at that age, the flute represented a feminine instrument, which is, I suppose, not an un-common perception.

Even more critically, Miles was introduced by a fellow choral misfit to the world of rock music, and from that point his world changed. Miles implored me for an electric guitar and (guilty again) I was not imme-diately enthusiastic. My new partner Baz, however, was more understanding, and in what Milly now recalls as the Christmas present that changed her life, he bought her the longed-for instrument. And just like that, the full power of Miles's musicianship was unleashed.

Suddenly, he realised that he could make music by listening, copying, experimenting and composing, rather than being confined by other people's ideas of what and how he should play. Miles worked obsessively to begin to master the guitar and devoured every type of music. But the heavier it was, the better. The rage, anguish and sheer cataclysmic noise of hard rock somehow unlocked the anger and despair that had frozen him emotionally, and now, although still in retreat, that retreat was inside a cocoon of music that brought him meaning and release.

I, on the other hand, was no closer to understanding the underlying cause of Miles's unhappiness, and it weighed upon me constantly.

CHAPTER 3

I asked Milly recently what she remembered as the low points of her early years. Without hesitation, she answered, '1992 to 2015', or, in other words, from the day she was born to the day she eventually came out. She had been depressed for her whole life, and with every passing month, as her awareness of herself, her body and the world around her became more acute, her depression only grew worse. I now know that this kind of suffering is a way of life for most, if not all, trans people – and that they suffer depression not *because* they are trans but because their lives are so often beset by struggles with confusion and shame, and in many cases by a painful catalogue of abuse and oppression. Their suicide risk is catastrophically high. Studies have found that around 84 per cent have contemplated suicide and, shockingly, around 45 per cent have attempted it. Painfully, that number included Miles. Before they transition, trans people typically suffer from gender dysphoria (an acute sense of being in the wrong gender) and body dysmorphia (a sense of horror at the body they find themselves inhabiting), leading to crushing feelings of isolation, anxiety and despair. Often, they describe feelings of moving beyond depression into a state of numbness and disconnection with everything around them; as Milly said to me later, 'I felt completely dead inside.' Stories of the burden of depression that trans women and men endure are all heartbreakingly alike, and I recognise my daughter in all of them – now. But during those years, as she grew from a child to a young adult, I felt at a loss either to understand or to fix the constant aura of sadness she carried about herself.

Miles, apart from his obvious unhappiness, was socially anxious and avoided eye contact with most people, even those closest to him. As I now know, this is common to many trans people before they transition. Being addressed by their given name or required to state their assigned birth gender, for example on a form or over the phone, can cause crippling anxiety and even panic attacks. It was not only in choir that Miles kept his eyes down and his mouth closed; at school and at home he was regularly reprimanded for looking at the floor, mumbling and slouching. I realise now that this was his attempt to fade into the background, to avoid being seen and heard at all, rather than to have to be present in such a state of discomfort and 'wrongness'.

Miles's sensory system seemed oddly shut down too. He had no interest in food apart from a basic need for sustenance, his ability to differentiate colours and his sense of smell were both poor, and he appeared to find no pleasure in the little things of life; a sunny day, a beautiful place or a funny moment rarely brought a comment or even a smile. I have learnt since that this is another common manifestation of transgender depression. Many trans people report a sense of living life as if they were merely observing it in a kind of grainy black and white, and will often talk about their post-transition life as an explosion of sensation. When I first read Jan Morris's *Conundrum* I was struck by her description of exactly such an experience when she made the revelatory discovery of the simple enjoyment of the feeling of the sun on her skin or the breeze in her hair. Morris is eloquent when she speaks of this physical and emotional unveiling, and when I returned to *Conundrum* in the light of my own experiences as a travelling companion on the transgender journey, I was struck by the parallels between the way she expressed these changes in herself and what I have heard and learnt directly from my daughter. Milly tells me that after fully transitioning she now, for the first time, really 'sees' life in colour and fully experiences emotional depth. 'Even sadness is now a good feeling for me,' she says, 'because it means that I'm truly alive in myself. Finally, I *can* feel.' The joyous possibility of gender euphoria is the antithesis of that depression and dissociation that so many trans people endure as they try to find their way to a new life of hope, to their own self-validated future.

Puberty is an emotional and physical disaster for anyone with gender dysphoria. It doesn't require much insight or imagination to realise that the time when the body is blossoming into full adult physicality is extremely confronting and distressing to someone who wants to avoid exactly that. The desire to stop the process of physical maturity then becomes a desperate (and hopeless) battle of the mind against the body and, in the absence of other options, eating disorders are the weapon of choice. Despite its stereotype as an illness largely affecting affluent teenage girls, anorexia is actually four times as prevalent among trans teenagers as it is in the general population. Young trans people of both genders frequently impose rigid rules on their relationship with food, restricting calories to try to stop the development of feminine curves or to lose weight in order to appear more petite, delicate and less muscular. The obsessive monitoring of food intake also gives an illusion of control over something that is beyond control, and that obsession itself all too easily spirals into a dangerous place.

As with everything on my journey with Milly, hindsight is a fine thing. If I had known *why* my child was depressed instead of just knowing that she *was* depressed, I might have been able to do something (and yes, of course I tried doctors, counsellors, housemasters and psychiatrists – even organists). If I had understood the revulsion she felt at the physical changes burgeoning in her XY-chromosome body, I might have had an inkling as to why she veered from one bizarre and worrying diet to the next. But I was lost in the dark – though at least I do know she didn't confide in anyone else either. I console myself slightly with the thought that it was not my failure alone. By the time Miles left choir school at thirteen, it was obvious to me that my child was fading away. I knew something was seriously wrong.

Miles's disconnection from life remained all but impenetrable. The only thing that reconnected the wires was his immersion in the virtuoso guitar-led music of Iced Earth, DragonForce and Yngwie Malmsteen. As his fascination with this music grew, the spectrum of his listening, playing and writing expanded rapidly into new styles, and he became obsessed with jazz guitar. Charlie Christian, Wes Montgomery, John Scofield, Allan Holdsworth and many others became household names to me. I could now tell bebop from post-bop as easily as I could Bach from Beethoven. Although Milly and I don't necessarily see eye to eye on matters of musical taste and listening pleasure, I quickly learnt that the virtuosity of these jazz musicians was the equal of any in my own classical world. I was fascinated by the rhythmic extremes they explored, by the harmonic complexity of the music, by their challenge to musical boundaries. I was also amazed at the way Miles could transcribe and play anything he heard. Nonetheless, Miles's passion for guitar-led jazz was just one more thing about him that didn't fit in the box, and as he entered his final year in the choir his mental health worsened under the pressure to focus on more conventional musical and academic pursuits.

In the last year at every choir school, all attention turns to Common Entrance and the very real possibility of a music scholarship at a major public school. This path is well trodden for good reasons. Leaving the cloistered environment of a choir school at nearly fourteen, with an education grounded in Latin and the liturgy, a chorister has spent the past six years in a cassock and surplice and will probably be more in tune with Rose and Byrd than R&B. Most parents take the view that late entry to the local comprehensive might be a culture shock too far. In any case, public school music departments are hungry for top choristers and, for the right candidate, fees need not be an obstacle. Although they move up to secondary school on the cusp of losing their treble voice, the musical grounding of a choral education means that former choristers are likely to be valuable instrumentalists in the school orchestra and, at the very least, useful tenors and basses in the chapel choir. With luck, the school might even get a year of 'the voice' for that choir before the inevitable

squawk happens. And so, in gold ink on polished ma-
hogany boards around the school dining hall the names
and destinations of those who have gone before are
inscribed: Eton, Harrow, King's School Canterbury,
Rugby, Uppingham, Winchester. The roll call of glory
and expectation.

Miles was desperate to escape the choir and start
afresh in a school where he could at least imagine
the possibility of happiness. He began to practise the
flute ardently and even prepared the required audition
song with something approaching willingness. He was
clearly hoping for something transformative in his new
school and, although I was delighted by this positive
improvement, I was not sure what was driving his burst
of optimism. Lucas was at a boys' school, but Miles had
firm ideas of his own. He wanted to go to a school with
girls. In fact, he refused to consider anything else. And
so, very much against his father's wishes, we settled on
a school that offered full co-ed boarding. I was rather
pleased with his choice, thinking it showed a promising
interest in the opposite sex and perhaps an indication
that he might be finding other interests in life. I did not
realise, of course, that Milly wanted to go to a school
with girls because she *was* a girl.

The abusive misogyny of my now ex-husband, however, had not lessened over time, and Milly's determination to enjoy a life with girls in it unleashed his
father's full, impotent vitriol. Day after day he reduced

Milly to tears with demands and insults over his choice of school, turning up at the boarding house to berate staff and pour his wrath on Milly. Only a top-tier boys' public school met his own ego-driven definition of success for his children; in his eyes, Milly was a failure, and I was the cause of it. Nonetheless, Milly stood firm. Nothing swayed his unshakeable desire to move into a sphere where he could start to imagine and tentatively experience life as a girl.

This implacable refusal was the first outward instance of the courage Milly has shown all through her trans journey and, for me, the first time when I knew I had to stand with my child to protect and support her as she reached for something (I did not know what) deep inside herself.

The more his father pushed, the more Milly was resolute in his determination to succeed in the coming auditions. The guitar was reluctantly but firmly put aside while Handel and Poulenc received some overdue attention on the flute, and by January, Miles was destined for his chosen school on a full music scholarship. Into a boys' boarding house, of course, but also, at last, into a school where (I know now) her secret hope was that by living side by side with girls she might have the opportunity to start the journey towards a female life. So much of what happened at that school I only found out later, but, once there, it didn't take long before I noticed Miles's optimism had been replaced by deepening despair. And then one evening I received a desperate email from Milly in which he confessed that he had been cutting himself and had attempted suicide by electrocution in the boarding house. I drove up in the middle of the night for an urgent conference with the housemaster; but even then the truth of the matter was obscured. Milly was a misfit, he said, intelligent but academically lazy, talented but uncooperative. Always in the music block, never in the common room. Probably just playing up because he had been sent out of class for some misdemeanour or other. What? I asked. 'Nothing worth mentioning,' the housemaster said. 'Teenage boys, you know. Got to expect the odd bit of trouble, eh?' In fact, again long after the event, I learnt that the detention was for wearing makeup to class, that Milly had been sent out and that later that same housemaster had unleashed a withering homophobic diatribe upon her at lunch, in front of the assembled house. No wonder he glossed over it. No wonder Milly was driven to the edge.

In spite of this, Milly was adamant he wanted to stay in school. He was thriving musically and participating in every available opportunity: orchestra, wind band, chamber ensemble, chapel choir, a cappella choir, big band, cadet air force band. He filled every free moment with music, and at least that kept him away from his tormentors. It took me ten years to discover the truth. At home, Miles kept his body covered. I had not seen him even in swimming trunks since he was a young child. But one day, not long after Milly had come out,

I inadvertently walked into her bedroom as she sat in a towel combing her long hair. Across her back I saw livid scars, like healed carpet burns or lashes. Shocked, I asked her what on earth had happened to cause this. 'School,' she said abruptly. 'I can't talk about it.' I still know no more.

I do know, though, that in her first year at school, now having a large circle of girl friends, she borrowed their uniform (a skirt and blouse) and wore them to class. Her punishment was severe, but I was not informed. 'It just seemed natural to me,' Milly told me later. 'I was only fourteen. I really didn't see why it was wrong.' With the help of her new friends, Milly also began to experiment with makeup. She had decided that the only way to cope with the strange dichotomy of her experiences and desires was to identify as gay, and she became the cross-dressing pet of the girls' boarding house, where they taught her how to apply eyeshadow and played with her hair. A request for ballet lessons soon followed, and Milly took on the school authorities to be allowed to join a ballet class. My admiration for this, even then, knew no bounds, and we had fun shopping for ballet pumps at Freed in Covent Garden. In those pregnant imaginary conversations, so long ago, I always hoped for a daughter who loved ballet.

You could be forgiven by now for thinking I was rather slow on the uptake – except for one thing. Milly had become a bodybuilder. By the time Milly left choir school, I was anxiously aware of his failing physique. He barely ate, and the effort even of opening a door taxed him. I could see every rib, and school trousers needed adjustment to stay on his bony hips. By the third year at secondary school, all this had changed. Milly was exercising obsessively and had been given permission to be on the special 'sports diet'. Extra protein at supper. First chance at the seconds. A free pass to the gym. Milly's day revolved around just two things: music and muscle. He was as extreme in his devotion to weights as he was to the guitar. Now no one could mess with Milly.

I asked her not long ago if this change from anorexic to the gym king of the lower sixth was not strangely inconsistent with her desire to be more feminine. She told me that of course it was, but not only did her newly muscular build now give her protection from the relentless physical bullying, the exercise also helped contain her depression. By now, she had been on antidepressants for some time and was seeing the counsellor at school every week, so finding something that helped her cope with her own inner torment on a day-to-day basis was a huge step forward. It was also a desperate last-ditch attempt to try to reconcile her gender with her body. Not knowing that anyone else in the world shared her condition, or that there was any possible way to change the body to fit her mind, she hoped that if she made that body the epitome of manliness she might somehow 'become' the body she had created.

Ten years on, this is a reminder of how much the world has changed. It is inconceivable today that a teenager in Milly's predicament might be ignorant of the options. The fact that she found her way to femininity without early exposure to any ideas about transgenderism gives the lie to the all-too-commonly held notion that the media and LGBT education in schools are creating a fashionable transgender contagion among young people. Having travelled this path with my daughter, I now know that no one, absolutely no one, would choose the gruelling road to transitioning unless the utmost desperation drove them there.

CHAPTER 4

The expression 'coming out' has a sense of announcement and movement about it, of a moment in time that can be clearly marked. One day you are in a room (or indeed a closet) behind a closed door; the next, you have pushed against that door and there you are. Out. With fanfare or without, there is a defined point of change; or at least that is what I had always imagined. Except that, in reality, coming out is more of a process than an event, and I have come to think of it instead as a passage from darkness into light. The path is rocky in places, slow-going at times; there are friends and enemies who may either help or ambush you along the way, moments when you dare to dream of the possibility of beautiful vistas ahead, and other long, hard miles where there seems little hope of ever seeing daybreak over the horizon. Everyone's personal coming out story is different, of course, but when you finally discover that your child is trans and you decide to walk with them, coming out becomes your journey too.

The way we tell those stories to ourselves and to others reshapes the narrative of our lives. It throws everything you thought you knew about the person you have loved from the day they came into the world into disarray. Fond childhood memories are now revealed to be built on quicksand. If I remember a lovely afternoon picnic, a small island of happiness in a shade-dappled park, my daughter remembers the sharp pang of being expected to join in the rough and tumble of the playing field when she just wanted to be left alone, to look for conkers or watch the squirrels. If I proudly think of the day I saw her receive the Air Training Corps Sword for top RAF cadet, her memories are of throwing herself heart and soul into the Combined Cadet Forces in a desperate attempt to make herself the boy she wasn't. And when I think of the choir years, imagining my child surrounded by the beauty of the music and the soaring stones of the chapel, that child remembers with undying fury the verses that she heard as a constant antiphon of hatred against difference, a litany of homophobia. 'If a man lies with a man, as he lies with a woman, both of them have committed an abomination,' the voices from the pulpit told her. 'Men committed shameful acts with other men, and received in themselves the due penalty for their error.' It was quite clear to Milly that there was no place for her in the kingdom of God whose praises she had to sing daily, and she despised and was mortally wounded by all their words. She heard them as an attack on the depths of her being. 'Male and female created he them.'

The way that the inner knowing of being transgender emerges is as varied and unique as the individual. The 'wrong body' narrative has become the dominant model for understanding transgenderism in our society: the idea of being 'trapped' is something we can all understand and so is an easy shortcut to expressing the complexities of gender and its relationship to the physical form. It also allows us to make amends with our own discomfort at this strangeness by offering a solution. You're trapped? We have a way to help you escape. With the assistance of medical science you can be like us, a cisgendered individual, a person whose sense of self matches the shape of the flesh. For many, this particular road to self-actualisation is exactly what they long for. It is very common to hear trans people describe their sense of being 'wrong' from the earliest age, and I now know that this was Milly's experience. Her defining memory is of being four years old, huddled under the climbing frame in intense negotiation for a role in a game of superheroes, where she knew with untrammelled certainty that she wanted to be Batgirl – that she *was* Batgirl. She didn't know that the unspoken rules of the playground would soon make that impossible, but, then, in those days of innocence, Batgirl she was.

Others, though, experience years of anxiety, despair and repression before they acknowledge their gender identity even to themselves. For those people there are as many shades of transition as there are of coming out. In fact, only around 33 per cent of trans men and women undergo full surgical transition through genital reconstruction; most others are happy somewhere on a spectrum which ranges from aesthetic presentation in their gender identity, through different stages of medical transition (hormone therapy), to partial surgery (such as having the Adam's apple shaved to make it less prominent). Such people make easy pickings for verbal assault in the TERF wars of trans-exclusionary radical feminism, but I prefer the gentler wisdom of Jan Morris, who, in reflecting on her own experience, wrote,

> I never did think that my own conundrum was a matter either of science or of social convention. I thought it was a matter of the spirit, a kind of divine allegory, and that explanations of it were not very important anyway. What was important was the liberty of us all to live as we wished to live, to love however we wanted to love, and to know ourselves, however peculiar, disconcerting or unclassifiable, at one with the gods and angels.

The night Milly finally revealed her true self, there was an almighty family row, or, as Lucas might have it, a vigorous and uncompromising intellectual debate. Tensions were already running high around the kitchen table. Lucas and his new wife, Serena, were home for Christmas from Sydney, where he was now studying law; Milly's girlfriend, the quirky, purple-haired Leigh, had just arrived from her family home in New Haven, Connecticut; and my brother, Chris, had flown in from Perth. Milly and Leigh had met at a wedding a year or so earlier and to my surprise had immediately become an item. Until now, Milly had very much kept relationships private, though I knew that various people came and went in his personal life, but for some time I had thought he was gay – mainly because he had told me he was. Against the background of Milly's declared sexual orientation, therefore, this new and serious relationship with Leigh left me rather nonplussed. On the other hand, I was by now used to the rollercoaster of Milly's complex nature, and I could see the positive effect that Leigh was having on his happiness.

It had been several years since Milly, home from school for the weekend, had, with eyes resolutely to the floor, walked into the kitchen, where he awkwardly pressed a scrap of paper into my hand. I was stirring a ragù. Strange how it is the small details like this that irrevocably anchor our most striking memories. 'I am gay,' the note read. I kept my concentration on the gently simmering sauce, tasting and seasoning as I began, clumsily and hopelessly, to try to say the words that might show that I was accepting, that I loved him regardless, always. I did try that day, but still I said so many things that were hurtful, lacking in understanding, wrong. The love was there, but in self-awareness and real acceptance I was lost. I did not acknowledge the years of hidden pain that had brought Milly to this point; nor did I feel genuine empathy for the shame and desperation that had been threaded through her life – and which I had in many ways compounded by choices I had made and imposed on her. I responded carelessly and with clichés to her anguished revelation, feeling self-satisfied with how I accepted the news. I know now that in truth I failed. Now that I have reflected on those days with honesty, I think I was mainly relieved for myself, happy to have some kind of explanation for Milly's years of isolation and depression. I grasped enthusiastically at the relatively easy next step of simply re-cataloguing my child as 'my gay son' and thought little further on the subject. With a new label for Milly, I could put a tick in this convenient box and move on. It felt like progress at the time. I know now that my response that day left Milly feeling that home was still not a safe place to declare herself fully, and for that I take responsibility and feel the deepest regret.

And so it was Christmas, and at last my family were all here. I had been looking forward to this reunion for weeks, filling the fridge with champagne and treats, baking homemade hams and mince pies and feeding my great-grandmother's Christmas pudding recipe with extra brandy. Food and the pleasures of cooking had always been the touchstone of our family celebrations, and on Boxing Day, with the indulgences of the festive dinner just one day behind us, the kitchen was still full of good things. Now they all lay untouched. On Christmas night, Baz, by now my husband of some ten years, had been rushed to hospital by ambulance after he collapsed suddenly on the living room floor, shaking and gibbering uncontrollably. None of us had more than a few hours' sleep as we took it in turns to pace up and down in A&E while test after test came back negative. Some kind of infection? Malaria? Blood poisoning? I kept vigil at the hospital all night and long into the next day as Baz was transferred first to a medical ward, then to an isolation ward for unidentified infectious diseases, until eventually my brother came to tear me away. 'You'll be no good to anyone unless you get some sleep,' he said. 'They don't know what's wrong and there's nothing you can do right now. You need to come home. I know this isn't the Christmas you'd planned, but at least we're all here together.' I left Baz plugged into monitors and full of tubes, fighting against attempts at sedation and infusions of vitamin B12 as he continued to hallucinate wildly, and headed home under Chris's gently insistent hand for some much-needed food and rest.

Back in the warmth of the Christmas kitchen, we all sat fretfully at the table. The mood was restive.

Everybody was, in varying degrees, tired, anxious and hungry, lacking the motivation even to put leftovers on a plate. A desultory attempt was made at Scrabble (could there be a more middle-class response to a crisis?) which was soon abandoned in favour of a round of Bananagrams from someone's Christmas stocking. Milly was annoyed by Lucas's ruthlessly competitive approach and withdrew into himself, noodling incessantly on the guitar that was never out of his hands, until the game petered out in an atmosphere of weariness and niggles. Half-hearted attempts at conversation filled the gaps, though I was constantly on the alert for the sound of the phone and the hope of positive news.

'What's your view on the Ministry of Justice review on whether trans women should be sent to male or female prison, Mum?' Lucas had clearly decided a new, non-hospital-based topic of conversation was needed.

'I haven't really been following it,' I mumbled vaguely. Lucas's forays into current affairs always required a rapier-sharp response and no-excuses intellectual engagement. His Oxbridge-honed predilection for the cut and thrust of academic argument and his forensic legal mind meant any ill-considered opinion was received with excoriating counter-argument, and I could smell a debate brewing. Right at this moment, I just didn't have the energy.

'Tara Hudson,' he said. 'She's convinced the prison

authorities to transfer her from HMP Bristol to a women's prison in Gloucestershire.'

Milly was suddenly roused from his guitar reverie. 'She's lived all her life as a woman. She's been through years of hormone therapy and surgery. She's got the physique of a woman. Of *course* she should be in a women's prison,' he said angrily.

'*She*, in inverted commas, is a known violent offender,' Lucas replied. 'What about the physical and emotional safety of vulnerable women in prison? Why should trans rights take priority over women's rights?' Lucas would not let this argument lie, and now he was angry too. He turned to me.

'Do you think a trans woman is really a woman? Even a post-operative one? Should she have access to women's spaces? Just because she identifies as a woman should she be privileged with the status of actual womanhood?' I really didn't want this discussion now and, in truth, until this moment hadn't actually considered the issues except in the most fleeting way. I had not previously felt any particular necessity to form a definitive position on the nuances of third-wave feminism or current trans issues, and never less so than right now. But Lucas was intent on a resolution to this debate.

'Is she really a woman, Mum? You're a woman. Defend your position.'

I was exhausted and knew that a few miles away my

husband was in a critical condition, fighting an illness that eluded identification or treatment. I just wanted to be left alone. 'Umm, yes … I don't know.' Stop the argument. Agree with Lucas, have a shower and a cup of tea, go to bed. Sleep for a few hours. Go back to the hospital. I was craven. 'Alright, yes, I agree with you. I think that a self-identifying trans woman could potentially be a danger to women in a female prison.'

'So you're saying she's not a woman?'

'Yes.'

I would like to say that at this point I immediately reconsidered and instead stood up for the experiences of trans people, that I showed empathy and insight, that I understood their struggles and the oppression they have faced. But, stressed beyond endurance by everything that had fallen around my ears in the past twenty-four hours, vulnerable in the expectation of unknown trials ahead and lazily recollecting some opinion piece I'd read earlier, I let forth with comments that I now find unforgiveable. Crazed with tiredness and grief, I said so many things that today I would not, and I know that my carelessly judged comments left a deep fault line in my relationship with Milly that lingers still. As my daughter would say, 'The axe forgets, but the tree remembers.' But today I do remember, and my regret for the pain I caused my daughter that night is profound.

At my words, the ever-present accompaniment of the guitar stopped abruptly, leaving a hole in the air around us, and Milly shouted angrily, 'You don't know anything! I've got friends like that, friends in London. You've got no idea what their life is like.' Milly stormed out of the room, flushed with fury, closely followed by Leigh. I was at a loss to know what had caused this outburst and such obvious distress but knew better than to run after them. Like me, Milly drew his space around himself and any attempt at talking would not be welcomed. Lucas, on the other hand, seemed satisfied with having won my agreement to his logical position – for him, intellectual honesty is paramount – and he and Serena drifted off to their room with supportive words about Baz and tomorrow's hospital visiting plans.

I sat alone in the kitchen after my brother, too, had said goodnight, and tried to gather my thoughts. The past thirty-six hours had been an ordeal of relentless anxiety, stress and physical exhaustion, and that was now compounded by an undercurrent of tension with Milly and Leigh that I couldn't fathom. It was very late, and I took comfort in the quiet and impenetrable dark of the countryside. A heavy frost had fallen on our small Cambridgeshire village and nothing disturbed the second night of Christmas but the soft hoot of a barn owl nearby and the occasional bark of muntjac deer in the hedgerows. And so I felt, rather than heard, Milly's soft footsteps on the stone floor as he moved silently through the doorway behind me and into the kitchen. 'There's something I need to tell you…' he said. I looked up and saw one emotion after another draw its trail across Milly's fine-boned face. Tears brimmed, catching in his extraordinary, luxuriant eyelashes before trickling down his cheeks; anger flashed briefly in his eyes, replaced as quickly by anguish. For once, he was looking straight at me. 'I'm transgender. I have always wanted to be a woman. And I can't go on any longer like this. I've made an appointment with the doctor.' I didn't hear much more. Words like Gender Identity Clinic swirled around confusingly in the midnight silence.

I wish I could say that at that moment the scales fell from my eyes, all became clear and I joyfully embraced my child and her revelation, gifted with a clear vision of how life would now change for the better. The truth is that my first thought was 'Why are you doing this to me now? Haven't I got enough on my plate tonight?', though I retained enough presence of mind as I staggered under the weight of this new information not to actually let those words escape. Instead, leaning forward against the sink, an unconscious support against my tiredness and shock, I stared out into the pitch darkness of the wintery garden and managed to stumble onward.

'How long have you known?' I asked.

'Always.'

'But you never said anything. All these years. So much unhappiness, so much counselling. Why didn't you tell me?'

'You're just about the last person I've told. All my

friends know, everyone at college.' As I said, coming out is a process, and not everyone is offered that trust at the same time. I was sad then not to have been worthy, but it has taken deep reflection over time to begin to understand why. Why my daughter had felt so isolated, so lonely, so afraid; the endless mistakes small and large that I had made and that had left her feeling unsafe and unheard; the inescapable truth of never having been the mother I had hoped I was.

'And Leigh?' I asked.

'Yes, of course, Leigh knows.'

'But... but...' I don't think I've ever felt more of a failure or less in tune with the moment. I struggled to regain my equilibrium and reach towards some kind of normal to hang onto, shipwrecked as I was in this storm which had swirled in, unforeseen, out of the darkness.

We sat down at the table on the same chairs we had been sitting in a few hours earlier when Lucas's gender-critical analysis, and my complicity in it, finally collapsed the fragile survival structure that Milly had constructed around her life. Years of repressed pain poured out in a torrent of angry words. Already I knew that I needed to allow myself to be swept along on this tidal wave of grief and fury, to take the blame even if, at that time, it felt grossly unjust. Instinct told me that Milly was just beginning to purge a lifetime of anguish, and if I was in the firing line, so be it. I asked again why she had not felt able to tell me sooner, when she knew that I had constantly tried to find answers to ease her clearly troubled life, visiting counsellors and doctors with her time and time again. Her answer was bewildering. 'Because you're a homophobe. And apparently, as you've made clear tonight with Lucas, you're a transphobe too.'

'I... what? How can you say that?'

'But you are. The things you've said, the way you've listened but never really heard. You think you're not a homophobe because you've got gay friends, and that's true but it's not a defence. You have never reached into understanding my life or recognised what I was suffering. Even when it's been in front of you, you've never heard my cry. I didn't feel safe. Home was not a safe place for me.'

Milly's face was cracked with pain, her lips trembling, a lifetime of tears in her eyes. I was devastated. We talked long into the night, soon joined by Leigh, who had quietly padded into the kitchen and become part of the conversation. The vortex of Milly's despair and fury began to ebb, and so too did the first waves of my shock. I was shivering from head to toe as my body succumbed to the onslaught of stress, emotional turmoil and the utter physical and mental exhaustion of the past day and a half. 'In spite of all my failings, I do love you and support you, Milly, and I always have, even though I see now that it hasn't been good enough,' I said. 'I know it's hard for you to believe at the moment, when you are dealing with everything you have suffered, and it's going to take me a while to get things right, but I *will* get things right. I don't know what any of this involves right now, but I promise things will change. I will change. I will be there for you, whatever it takes.'

Her tears were silent now and I watched them run gently down her cheeks. 'I often wear girls' clothes,' she offered tentatively. 'I keep them hidden in my wardrobe.'

'I'd love to see how you look,' I said. 'Could you show me?' I knew that Milly was experimenting by prodding for a tender spot, a place where we might start the process of engagement, and where I might at last see her as she wished to be seen. She glanced at me anxiously and without a word disappeared upstairs with Leigh. 'I'll be down in a minute!' she called behind her. Five minutes later, my daughter entered the kitchen. Her hair was pushed up into a messy bun, showing off a pair of pretty earrings. Her legs were long and shapely in opaque tights and boots, and she wore a miniskirt and black polo neck jumper, with enhancements that gave her a womanly form. She was beautiful. I was stunned, but, most of all, my heart leapt to see the sheer naturalness of the smile that spread across her face. We held each other tight and, although I had no idea where we were going, I knew that our journey had begun.

CHAPTER 5

So, I thought, when I awoke after a few hours of fitful sleep, the only thing I could do was begin with a single step. I now knew this journey of a thousand un-imagined miles was the road that I would have to travel, and if an ancient Chinese proverb was the most useful advice I could summon in my dazed state then it would have to do. But at that moment I couldn't even conceive what the first step might be. I lay in my strangely empty bed and stared at the ceiling, cataloguing my thoughts. Item one: Baz was in hospital, in a critical condition, cause unknown. Might die? Don't think about that. Not today, not yet. Item two: I now have a daughter. Who, admittedly, still looks exactly like the son I had yes-terday. Apart from the miniskirt and so on, obviously. Might she end up in a Moroccan hospital having some barely credible physical reconstruction? (Jan Morris was still my only point of transgender reference.) No, don't think about that either. Definitely not today, and preferably not ever. I needed a plan, and for that, no matter what life has thrown at me, the library has always been my refuge. And so, I decided, still contemplating the ceiling, I would read my way through this. I would consult the consultants and I would seek out whatever gender-related biographies and histories and ethnographies I could find and shake them until they revealed their stories to me. And most of all, I would talk and talk and talk to my daughter, until I could pull some meaning and understanding from the heart of this emotional whirlpool, which I feared might otherwise pull me under, drowning me in its disorientating waters.

There are a lot of ways of telling the transgender story, and I am very aware that the trans community may justifiably consider that I am not the person to do it. In terms of the profound knowledge of being and living, they are right. My only qualification is my own life as I have lived it and the experience I have gained vicariously through my daughter. Knowing the number of egregious errors I have made along the way, the times I've hurt my child with careless words, and the misconceptions I have been slow to acknowledge and change, it has taken me a long time to even muster the credibility of being considered a trans ally. But I am my daughter's ally, out and proud, and I have gained deep empathy and respect for trans people, wherever they might be on their own road to fulfilment. In writing about my thoughts and experiences, I make no claim to speak for these fellow travellers; they have their own voices, and increasingly those voices are being heard. But by writing from a perspective which recognises that being trans is a confusing and confronting concept for those of us who have the good fortune to inhabit a body that easily co-exists with the mind, and by reflecting upon what I have learnt along the way, I hope that I might in some small way add to the diversity and richness of that story.

So far, all I knew was that my daughter had experienced her whole life as a female in a male body. 'For as long as I can remember, I always wanted to be a girl,' she told me. This was my first philosophical hurdle, as I could not imagine what such an unshakeable knowledge of inner femininity might actually mean. I am, in every aspect of myself, female, and yet I would say I have no idea what it means to 'know' I am a woman. I know what it is to be womanly, I know what my physical form is and the nature of my biological capacities, but as far as I am concerned these are very far from my defining characteristics. I can only be what I am inside my head, and from that place I only know what it is to be me. I ask myself how I can know if the way I think or feel is in some manner distinctively feminine? I have no other inner experience against which to compare it. So to me the idea that one might have an absolute and intrinsic sense of self as either male or female has been difficult to grasp. In this, I accept the lack is most likely mine, whether that be lack of imagination or whether I simply lack the experience. I do not doubt that others may have a fundamentally gendered (or mutably gendered) essence which it seems I am not aware of in my own life. I have always felt that I contain both masculine and feminine attributes, and I suspect that we all do, in different levels of balance. So I can only speculate that perhaps for many trans people the polarisation of their gender and physical body is the trigger for a kind of heightened self-awareness which has as much to do with an inner longing or discomfort as it does with any expression of socialisation or biology.

Many commentators embrace the construct of the 'third gender' when talking about trans people (and even more so about non-binary trans people), but as I began to read and explore I found that for me this idea was particularly unhelpful. It seemed to me that the idea of the third gender was, at least in Western society, really a way for others to corral the many varieties of trans bodies into a comfort zone that was convenient for them. As with so much of the trans narrative, I had begun to realise that it is the language of others – and the language of othering – that is allowed to stand in for the real and nuanced voices of lived experience. You say you're a man and, true, you have no breasts, but yet you also have no penis? Third gender. You say you're a woman but you battle against facial hair and have the sexual organs of a male? Third gender. I have come to understand that gender plurality is immensely more complicated than this, and I certainly know that my daughter would never accept this classification. It is not for us who have never experienced the social erasure of our very being to create a convenient filing system to define and categorise all the myriad ways that people can see and express themselves in their lives. Milly's way was to identify as a woman in a body that matched her inner sense of self, and the idea of relegation to the gender equivalent of some kind of demilitarised zone was as repugnant to me as it was to her. When Milly finally received her Gender Recognition Certificate and was able to expunge her birth details, replacing them permanently on record as female, she cried, overwhelmed with emotion as she crossed her personal finish line.

Another popular narrative is that indigenous cultures, untrammelled by the Judaeo-Christian tradition, have a natural understanding of gender fluidity, which they welcome, often endowing it with magical implications. Probably the most widespread of these is the Native American 'two-spirit' concept of sexual, gender and/or spiritual identity. In fact, the term 'two-spirit' was only adopted by American First Peoples in the 1990s to represent the spectrum of gender roles traditionally honoured within the various nations; its panlinguistic purpose was to create a single expression serving

all Native Americans that would counter the highly pe-
jorative term 'berdache' imposed upon them by colonial
anthropologists. The two-spirit trope has, however, been
culturally appropriated by some LGBTQ sympathisers
in mainstream Western culture, I suspect because its
other-worldly representation of the queer experience
appeals to a kind of spiritual vanity – a stance scathingly
quashed by Geo Soctomah Neptune, a Passamaquoddy
Two-Spirit, who points out that this sacred tradition
is *not* a poetic way for non-Native LGBTQ people to
express themselves.

Around the world, there are many societies that have
always accepted that there are females who naturally
display overtly masculine traits, and males who embody
feminine ones. In most cases, they are recognised early
in life as having innate characteristics that are not defined by their physical form and are brought up to live
openly as their acknowledged gender rather than their
biological sex. Very often, such people are regarded as
having special spiritual powers and perform ritual roles
in their society. The usual analysis of this is that the
masculine–feminine union they represent gives them a
divine 'wholeness' which others lack. I wonder, though,
whether it might also be that the very slipperiness of
their gender identity suggests to those around them that
they may be able, equally mysteriously, to pass through
other cracks in the fabric of the universe and commune
with the divine. For me, however, all these ideas were

interesting and novel but of little use in making sense of the new world I was navigating or of Milly's life as she was experiencing it. In fact, Milly strongly rejects any narrative that frames the trans journey as a spiritual quest and, having travelled with her through its very physical landscape, I can understand that.

My attempts to understand transgenderism, I soon began to realise, were taking me down a rabbit hole, and I spent weeks in Cambridge University Library, where I was lucky enough to have access to a whole world of scholarship and thought. I moved on to essays on gender and the body in medieval and early modern Europe, reading about female mysticism in the Middle Ages (where living and dressing as a man was positively received as an attempt by women to approach the masculine ideal of the Christian deity) and about the feminisation of the monastic language used to describe Christ (in the fabulously titled *Jesus as Mother* by Caroline Bynum). I learnt that, although there is no specific record of transgenderism as a concept in medieval sources, there are many early accounts of people leading transgender lives, as there were also in the ancient world. The evidence abounds that such inclinations have always existed, in every society.

And then, in a blinding flash of clarity, it occurred to me that none of this mattered. The pursuit of historical and anthropological evidence for transgenderism – by me, by the transgender community and by academics

– was a blind alley. It was fundamentally a search for validation and justification, a way of imploring the world, 'Please believe that I am transgender and my feelings are real; here is all the evidence that others across time and place have felt the same. As with them, so with me.' I asked myself, why should this be necessary? If just one person of all humankind needs to express their true self by presenting in another gender, why can we not just accept this? Suddenly my whole endeavour to understand transgenderism in this academic way seemed as ludicrous as trying to seek a philosophical proof of love. There's simply no need. If someone you care for deeply declares themselves to be female when their body tells you otherwise, why do we look to books to validate this before we can accept it? It mattered nothing to me that there might be a Hawaiian māhū somewhere who felt the same. I loved my daughter, and above all things I wanted her whole, happy and safe, to be the person she knew she was. It was *her* story I needed to be listening to.

But all that took place over many weeks and months; this morning my task was simply to find the strength to get up and face another day. It was time to go back to the hospital and put aside my bewilderment. Today, I needed to wear a different hat, pressing junior doctors, consultants and nursing staff for information and, I hoped, for solutions. I was fighting for Baz's life and the news was not good. Although the uncontrollable infection was showing signs of being tamed and Baz had stabilised overnight, the scans and blood tests and biopsies had thrown up a verdict. Baz was very seriously ill with a blood disorder that, even with the best possible spin put on it, was terminal. This week, next week, soon. Who knew? It was untreatable except with a regime of transfusions. I felt myself struggle numbly against the load of grief. I was going to lose my husband, just as surely as I was about to lose my son. The anguish wrapped itself around my chest, but, for both of them, I knew I had to hold fast.

Milly's revelation of the previous evening now weighed on me like another bereavement and, if anything, this morning the shock was worse than when she had first disclosed herself to me. Could it really have been only twelve hours ago? My heart reached out to my child and begged her back to the day before yesterday. I still wanted that little boy with his Thomas the Tank Engine and Buzz Lightyear, his Thunderbird rockets and Ninja Turtles, his blood-red surplice and snowy cassock, his guitars and weightlifting and Sword of Honour; but did I really, if that also meant the anorexia, the depression, the self-harm? Oh, Milly, forgive me. For your lifetime of pain and the burden of your sorrow, for the fact that you have spent twenty precious years not being seen, twenty long years crying out and not being heard. The poignant music of Thomas Tomkins's beautiful choral anthem 'When David heard that

Absalom was slain' came to my mind and clutched my heart: 'Oh Absalom, my son, my son, would that I had died for thee.' I knew how King David felt. The pain engulfed me, there in the shabby hospital café, and I quietly fell apart over my tepid, tasteless tea, overcome with silent grief.

That evening, Milly and I talked late into the stillness of the night. I was emotionally drained as one by one I heard her stories of cruelty and isolation, of living with fear, oppression and shame, and of, just sometimes, daring to hope. She talked to me of how, from childhood, she had always wanted to be a girl and of her attempts to explore and interpret in her own life what it meant to be feminine. For my part, I was confused, having first understood that Milly was gay, then encountering her blossoming relationship with Leigh, only now to find myself face to face with the revelation that my daughter was trans. Milly patiently explained that she was and always had been attracted to men, and that the love and support she felt in her relationship with Leigh had little to do with sexual attraction. She talked about the years of repression and confusion she experienced as she struggled to accept her gender identity and sexuality, attempting to compromise on the very essence of her being to try to fit in. But, she told me, it was never enough. She was not acceptable. The pain poured out into the space between us and I wondered if I could every truly cross it and meet this child I never knew I had.

Most of all, though, Milly talked about music. Music was the engine of Milly's being. From the day she first held a guitar her instrument had been her refuge and her voice, and it was only behind that barricade that she found any solace in the world. Milly's musicianship and virtuosic technique were starting to gather attention in London and even further afield, in Europe and the US. Now, she was paralysed by the thought that she might lose her career at the first whisper of her transition. The guitar is a very male instrument and guitar legends don't burn up the frets in a floaty skirt. But there was a deeper core to Milly's musical anxiety that had nothing to do with how she would be perceived. Her real fear, she confided, was that in some mysterious way her talent might be intrinsically linked to her deep unhappiness – the result of it, even – and, in the time-honoured narrative of the tortured artist, she worried that if she transitioned, that magical connection might be lost. She was pulled constantly between these two essentials, concerned that if she embarked upon hormone therapy, her mind and creative perceptions might alter with her body and, in turn, change the way she could express herself musically. This, Milly said, was the reason she had waited so long. She had convinced herself that her misery was in some way a source of her creativity, and she feared that in the process of gaining her feminine identity she risked losing her musical one. It had been an unbearable and insoluble dilemma, but the events of the past couple of days had tipped the balance. She could not go on.

The next morning Milly was dressed as she always had been in recent years: black band T-shirt (Dream Theater, probably), loose black jeans, black work boots and a black belt studded with rivets and looped with a chain. Nothing had changed in the rock and roll department, at least. I now knew that being seen as a long-haired musician had given her acceptable cover for the flowing hair that represented her femininity. Her passion for rock and jazz had not diminished in the years since choir school, though, and for now she was comfortable in public with the androgynous disguise it gave her.

'I need to tell Baz,' Milly said. 'Today.'

'He's too ill, darling. I'm not sure he will understand. Do you really think now is the best time?'

'It's absolutely the best time. I can't hide myself any more. It's *because* Baz is so ill. He's been like a father to me and I can't let him die without knowing who I am. It's time to be me. To everyone.'

I was moved by her clarity of purpose and by the rawness of her need for honesty. Her relationship with Baz as a stepfather, as I suppose is often the way, had not been straightforward, but at this crucial moment its depth was revealed. Baz had, after all, bought her her first guitar.

'And I'm going to tell Dad as well.'

This, I knew immediately, was a dreadful idea. I doubted Milly's father had changed very much in the ten years since I had last seen him, and I felt entirely confident that the news would not be well received.

'Are you sure that you really want to do that?' I asked. 'I'm afraid it might not go the way you hope.' The thought of Milly facing yet more hurt and rejection frightened me. Everything seemed so fragile right now.

'There's no choice,' she said. 'My life is not worth living like this. I am a shadow of myself, of who I need to be. I can't go on any longer. He's my father and he needs to know.'

At the hospital, Baz was weak, though more lucid than he had been. His imposing frame and vibrant personality had deflated to a heartbreaking husk, but today he was managing a little conversation. Milly had a guitar with her and sat by his bed quietly noodling. I knew that she was gathering her courage as she drew the soft chords around herself like a security blanket. The nurses didn't seem to mind, and the gentle music clearly brought Baz some pleasure too. He looked calmer and less frightened as Milly played. 'Baz, as you know, I've been unhappy for a long time. There is a reason for that.' She continued strumming as she spoke, never looking up from the guitar. 'I have always felt I was a girl and now I have decided to live my life as one.' I didn't know how Baz would respond; he was a good man, but this was a long way outside his rather conservative life experience. Milly had judged Baz well, though. A pragmatic approach was always best with him and he responded with equanimity.

'From now on,' she continued, 'I will be dressing as a girl and I will be changing my name. I would like you to refer to me as "she".'

Baz struggled weakly, pulling words down and letting them trail away. 'This… this… is surprising…' He tried again, stronger now. 'It's a new idea… new to me… I don't understand it. I will try to… to do the best I can.'

The conversation had clearly tired him, and the nurse encouraged us to let him rest. As we got up to leave, Baz attempted a fragile smile. 'You do look very pretty today.' From that day forward, Baz never once misgendered Milly.

Milly's second mission of the day was now looming, and I was anxious as she set off alone to see her father. At home, the hour passed slowly for me. I had been neglecting my brother and Lucas in the midst of the crisis, but they had gone out together in search of distraction and coffee. I nibbled on leftover turkey and had a glass of wine, rather earlier in the day than I usually allowed myself. Desperate times, desperate measures. It was dark when Milly finally walked through the door, and when I looked at her ashen face I didn't need to ask.

'He told me I am dead to him. He said…' she sobbed. 'He said, "You are no child of mine."'

CHAPTER 6

The process of outward change started slowly. For months Milly continued to dress as she always had, but gradually and almost imperceptibly she started to introduce tiny changes. First little hoop earrings appeared instead of the usual studs, then a more feminine style of jeans. A new T-shirt with a flattering, shoulder-slimming cut became a favourite, and she lavished her long hair with attention until it hung luxuriantly down her back. I sometimes wanted to brush its thick chestnut waves, though she never indulged me. I longed, I think, to feel, in some indeterminate but connected way, that I was part of the rebirth of this beautiful, bewildering person. As a mother, that mattered to me. These small transformations brought Milly both pleasure and extreme anxiety. She was not yet ready or comfortable to be seen at work dressed as a woman, but at the same time she needed to bring elements of that femininity to her daily life to remain true to her personal commitment to transitioning. The deliberately androgynous nickname that she had adopted as a seven-year-old – and which I had so signally failed to respect or understand – now served her well, but it was time to declare herself more plainly to the world. Milly was ready for a new name.

Nothing is more closely linked to our sense of identity than our name, and yet in most cases we ourselves have little choice in the name that represents us to the world. Given to us by loving parents, whether it is disappointingly ordinary or embarrassingly imaginative, five-in-every-classroom popular or unique in a perpetually irritating 'how do you spell that?' kind of way, our names are who other people think we are. And if that name doesn't match who *we* think we are? Well, then a name can be changed. The legal process of doing this is quite straightforward (less so the process of getting all your documents to agree with you), but the emotional process is far from it. Taking a new name for any reason is a life-changing decision and, like any such decision, there is usually much deliberation involved. For a trans person, though, this decision is even more freighted with meaning. It is likely to be the first public step they take in declaring their transition to the world, as well as a singular opportunity to reinvent themselves in their own image – an image they may have held inside for a lifetime. Many trans people go through a process of experimenting with the potential of their new name, trying on one alternative after another to see if they like the fit, before settling on a final choice and publicly declaring their new identity. For some, an ambiguous name feels more comfortable, perhaps because it allows for a less startling transition, whether internally or externally, while for others it is quite common to choose a name which in some way represents a symbolic aspect of their new freedom (Phoenix, say, or Dawn). Probably the most common option, though, is simply to adopt a feminised or masculinised version of the birth name, when there is one, moving seamlessly from George to Georgia, Charles to Charlotte, Samantha to Samuel. Less scope for confusion, and perhaps a vote of confidence in their parents' early choice and a recognition of the good intention originally at its heart, or so I like to think.

We talked a lot about the impending name change over a period of weeks while my daughter lived in a kind of suspended state in which 'Milly' was the only name she would answer to. If I inadvertently called her Miles – and at first that was a mistake I made all too often – angry words and tears would quickly follow. I now know that deadnaming is deeply hurtful and disrespectful, but when you've known someone all their life, as any parent will understand, in the absent-minded bustle of daily life you are as likely to make that slip as you are to call your child by the cat's name (surely it's not just me?). I worked hard to get it right, though, and these days have to check my own annoyance when others who should know better make the same mistake. Milly asked me what I might have called her had she been 'assigned female at birth' (I was quickly learning a new language too), and I cast my mind back to the days when I dreamt of that embryonic daughter. Eleanor, Lydia, Helena had all been in my mind then, but we both agreed none of those had a sense of rightness about it or matched the person she had become. In the end, Milly feminised her name in a way that also represented a new statement of her being. Miles was permanently abandoned, to live on only in occasional, unspoken family memories and old school reports, and Milly's ambiguous nickname remained as a useful constant. But, to start her new life, my daughter finally settled on Amelie, which she felt expressed the feminine alter ego of Miles. In its French origins the name means 'striving through hard work' and this spoke to her too: Amelie was at last striving towards becoming her true self.

New Year had come and gone, and Chris, Lucas and Serena had all returned to their own lives scattered across the world, none the wiser as to Milly's dramatic revelation. Leigh had gone back to university, and only Milly and I were left, holding tight to save each other from drowning in the tidal wave of trauma that had hit us both. Baz was still in hospital and I was spending long hours by his bedside, desperately trying to keep him tethered to this world and failing horribly. The illness had trigged a frightening mental breakdown, and his every waking hour was full of terrifying hallucinations and paranoia. Sometimes I would arrive to find him curled up against the top end of the bed, wrapped around and around in sheets and blankets so that only his eyes peered out. He trembled and whimpered, convinced that computer trolleys were gun turrets, or patients were spies, or that he was the protagonist in some kind of bizarre and inescapable theatrical production. I held his hand through agonising bone marrow biopsies and the search for veins as one after another collapsed, reassuring him constantly against his fears that doctors and nurses had malevolent intentions. He believed that the life-saving transfusions he was receiving were importing mind-controlling molecules into his system and that he was being prepared for organ harvest. Every day was an ordeal. It was utterly gruelling and exhausting, and much as I knew Milly's needs were desperate too, for once I put my foot down. 'I'm not being unsupportive,' I rebuffed Milly angrily in the face of her tears when I refused to host another kitchen table conference on the subject of coming out before the others departed. 'You know it's not often I say I can't cope, but right now I *am* saying that. I simply cannot handle any more stress. I need to stay strong for you and for Baz, and if Lucas or Chris or anyone else finds your news more than they can easily take on board, I don't think I would be able to deal with the conflict in a way that would protect and support you properly. I'm afraid I might just crumble.' Was it an excuse? Was I being selfish, blocking Milly's desperate need for acknowledgment and validation in favour of my own needs? Perhaps – or, more honestly, probably. I still had a long way to go towards understanding what my child had suffered. I knew Chris would be fine, just as surely as I knew Lucas would have a great deal to say about it all. A heated debate on identity politics was not something I could embrace with intellectual rigour or even-handed empathy at this time. Milly reluctantly agreed, though I now know I hurt her deeply. I think she could see I was barely on my feet and she knew she needed an ally now more than ever. We, or I, would break the news to the wider family once things had settled down a bit, however that was destined to be.

As the weeks went by, I began to worry once more about Milly's dysfunctional relationship with food and exercise. Since her secondary school days, in an effort to master the gender dysphoria that underlay the constant pain of her being, she had been obsessed by exercise and protein-intensive diets, and meals revolved around meat, meat and more meat, with added protein shakes just to make sure. Her unrelenting workout routine had given her an enviable physique – enviable, at least, if you happened to be a man. And now, suddenly, she was not. Having finally found the courage to align her outward appearance with her inner self, the iron biceps, muscular shoulders and hardened six-pack had to go. Milly's new priority was to try to reshape her body for a second time, and she ate constantly to try to increase her body fat-to-muscle ratio. But now she was unflinchingly vegan and she seemed to have no interest in either the taste or aesthetics of what she ate. Food was a purpose not a pleasure as she tried single-mindedly to lose the muscle she had built. An exercise bike appeared in the music studio, and whenever she wasn't practising she was on the bike, spinning for hours. I was beside myself with anxiety for her health all over again.

'Milly,' I said one day, unable to stay silent any longer, 'this can't be good for you. Please, please talk to me. What on earth are you trying to do?'

'I've got to create a calorie deficit,' she panted, not stopping for a moment. 'I'm trying to force muscle wastage. It's the only way to get rid of it, to reshape my body.'

'There's got to be a better way than this, Milly. It's dangerous. Crazy. It's incessant. Guitar, eat, bike, eat, guitar, eat, sleep, repeat. What about friends, what about life?'

'There is a better way,' she snapped, 'but right now I can't get it. Hormones. That's the only thing that will really start to change me, and until then I'm going to have to reduce my upper body by letting the muscles waste and balance it by building my thighs and hips.'

'So what do you need to do to get the hormones?' I asked. I didn't like the sound of this, but I was desperately worried as things stood.

'I'm on a two-year waiting list for an appointment at the Gender Identity Clinic in London.' This was news to me. I had no idea that her various doctor's appointments had gone so far and was shocked and saddened all over again at both her desperation and her lack of trust in my support. 'Right now, my body is not the shape of a woman,' she continued. 'I need to get to the point where I can go out dressed like a girl and not get pointed at or laughed at in the street. Or worse. Assaulted, abused, spat at. I need to be able to pass.'

The idea of 'passing' was a new one for me too, and I was horrified to hear those daily risks and the hurt she faced laid out so bluntly. I now understood Milly's dilemma, and her heartfelt wish to just fade away if things continued as they were still haunted my mind. I knew from our conversations that she had a private wardrobe of clothes which she had purchased online with Leigh's help (and she looked beautiful in the ones I had seen) but the idea of taking her new look into the open was still daunting. 'I think what I most need to start to pass is some coverage… the facial hair…' her voice trailed off in disgust. 'But I need to match my skin tone and I can't try on makeup in shops. Because right now, I don't pass.'

Once again, I felt downcast at my ineptitude in the face of so many painful and bewildering needs. I had not begun to consider all the daily challenges my child might be experiencing as she tentatively began this process of transitioning. Milly had as much right at the makeup counter as anyone else, and yet such an every-day outing presented a hopelessly impassable barrier. It might be trivial but perhaps, I thought, I could finally do something that would make a difference. Why could I not simply buy it for her? Milly had not yet been able to address the issue of her facial hair in a permanent way and, although she was obsessive about depilating, there was still a shadow that would be improved by some coverage. Foundation, we both agreed, would help. She already had lots of eyeshadows and nail polish, begged, borrowed and purchased online, and was possessed of the most enviable eyelashes which, unlike mine, would never require mascara; but a discreet base would make a difference. Milly has very different colouring to me so without testing samples the process of colour matching could only be guesswork. It was a conundrum: Milly was not ready to dress as herself in public but would be scorned, or at the very least looked at askance, if she presented at the counter with the appearance of a young man. And conversely, without effective foundation to conceal the telltale facial shadow, even in overtly female dress she would live with the constant anxiety of being outed as male-bodied.

There was only one solution.

'Hello,' I said to the terrifying makeup lady. 'I would like some advice on foundation.'

'Certainly,' she said. 'Now, you are very pale, so I think our No. 1 in Porcelain would be ideal.'

'No, it's not for me actually. It's for... it's for... my niece! Yes, a gift for my niece. But she's much more olive-skinned than me. Umm,' I improvised wildly, 'really very like your colleague. Do you think it might be possible to test it on her?'

Completely unperturbed, the makeup lady applied several different diagonal streaks of colour across her companion's cheekbones and blended them outwards to the jawline. 'This one is a good match. Sunkissed No. 4. Your niece will love this. Very good coverage but natural.' And just like that, it was done. Such a small step, such a trivial purchase, but perhaps one that would help Milly find the confidence to step outside, dressed as herself at last.

CHAPTER 7

For several months my life balanced precariously between two poles, and the energy ebbed and flowed between them as they competed for my attention. On the one hand, I was acutely aware of Amelie's need for support in this tremulous early stage of her new life; on the other, and there was no way to dress this up, Baz was dying. Between these extremes, I also needed to keep earning a living – more so now than ever, with Baz no longer capable of working – and my work, which in many cases had been in the diary for a year or more, meant I was travelling frequently. Baz was now home again and so, to the extent that I no longer needed to spend hours every day driving back and forth to the ward, sitting at his bedside and negotiating with doctors, things had improved somewhat. He was still very frail and his failing blood count left him constantly at risk of infections, but at least the psychosis was under control (mostly) and I did now feel able to leave him safely for a few hours at a time. Milly and I had become a care tag team, and between Baz and our various and erratic work commitments, daily life was a juggling act.

As always, I took refuge in music, and work was both my pleasure and my only respite. I still felt overwhelmed by sadness and anxiety, and the burden of responsibility for Baz's health and quality of life weighed heavily on me. I grieved for both of them. I also did not delude myself that, having changed her name and presentation, Amelie's transformation was now either settled or complete. I knew that Milly's desire for a full surgical transition meant that there were many serious issues ahead that we would need to confront and that there was a great deal more that I still didn't know or understand. For me, the journey was only just beginning, but as long as Baz remained reasonably stable at home, I hoped I might be ready to take the next step on that road with my daughter.

Milly was still dressing in her androgynous rock chick mode for work (which fortunately was in large part as an actual rock chick), but around friends and family and in anonymous situations she was now wearing a new and more obviously feminine style. Baz never failed to compliment her when she appeared at breakfast in a dress or a pretty top and, given that much of the time he was hallucinating cats or giant spiders or simply struggling to butter his toast, Milly was touched by his efforts. As she experimented with clothes and accessories in this controlled environment, Milly was moving towards presenting as a woman in small steps, and although it wasn't for my benefit I do think that made her metamorphosis easier for me. I guess incremental change is always less of a shock, whatever you are dealing with in life. She still carried huge anxiety about passing, though, and her need for reassurance was constant. Day after day I poured out a litany of comforting words, but there were many times when she couldn't even leave the house, so crippling was her fear of being exposed, ridiculed and humiliated.

'No, darling, I promise I can't see any beard shadow,' I would say.

'No, truly, your shoulders look perfect in that. No, no, really, they're not too broad. Yes, that jacket does balance them.'

'No, the shoes don't give it away. No, your feet look just the right size. You're tall, they're just in proportion.'

'You look lovely. No, I can't see your Adam's apple. Yes, you can definitely pass today.'

It was exhausting and demoralising. With every question, her apprehensions bubbled up to the surface, sometimes to evaporate, other times to paralyse. Then one day something occurred to me. Why did Milly have such a – how could I put it? – such a flat silhouette when she was wearing the skinny jeans she now favoured? Now that I thought about it, I realised she had looked like this for years. I was blindsided with an overwhelming sense, yet again, of my own failure to see.

Milly must be, I realised, somehow adjusting her body to achieve this more feminine shape, and I wanted to know more. I wanted to know so that I could be supportive, but also, if I'm honest, I wanted to know because these days I felt driven to try to understand what on earth was going on – in my life as much as hers. Milly's closely guarded privacy, though, would never allow that. I knew that for my daughter, passing discreetly and completely was her unfailing aspiration, and any attempt at such a conversation would be humiliating and intrusive. Not to mention how uncomfortable I might find it. I would have to satisfy my enquiry elsewhere, and this is how I came to learn about tucking.

For most trans women, the front line of conflict between their bodies and the world is, unsurprisingly, the shape of their genitals and the presence or absence of other secondary sex characteristics, such as the Adam's apple or breasts. All of these things can be altered surgically, but many choose not to, and even for those who do there is still a significant waiting period, during which the body is very often subdued and shaped by other means. It didn't take too much imagination to realise that Amelie's gently rounded breasts were moulded by a new bra enhanced with soft silicone inserts, but I hadn't really given any consideration to other aspects of her shape. I think it was because at this stage of her transition I was focused on coming to terms with her womanliness as an essence rather than as a physicality. Now, though, as I started to read, I had so many questions. I learnt that Milly was likely to be using a gaff. But was it painful? Dangerous? Damaging? As I worried for the physical well-being of my child I lurched wildly from bewilderment to anxiety.

A gaff, I discovered, is essentially an extremely tight jock strap designed to compress and conceal the genitals. Merely wearing one, however, is not in itself enough; there is considerable technique involved and, so I have discovered, many online tutorials to help trans women (and cross-dressers) acquire this arcane knowledge. Some trans women can manage without a gaff and instead tuck by stretching everything tightly backwards and taping it between the buttocks. Whether taping or using a gaff, the testicles pose a problem. The best tucking solution is to push the testes back inside the body rather than flattening them, so they reascend into the inguinal canal (again, handy YouTube videos are available). This sounded excruciating to me, but apparently once you have the knack it easily becomes a daily practice. When everything is properly positioned, the gaff is pulled up to hold everything in place. And if you need to go to the bathroom at some point during the day? I'm afraid that's going to be difficult or, if using tape, impossible. One rarely discussed trans health issue is the common risk of dehydration and urinary tract infections; all too often, trans women seriously restrict their fluid intake so that they can avoid the need to urinate and stay tucked all day. Most would rather face the possibility of dizziness, fainting, a racing heart and kidney disease than suffer the abhorrent sight of their own unwanted genitals and the potential humiliation of failing to pass in public.

The hard bit done, further improvements can be made to improve the body shape. The male body is typically an inverted triangle, broad at the shoulders and narrower at the hips, whereas the classically idealised feminine form is an hourglass, rounded at the breasts and hips and curving into a narrow waist. Once all is tucked away and prevented from escape, either by the gaff or by taping, some trans women will then add another undergarment to achieve the body shape they hope for, padding out the hips and bottom to achieve a womanly shape that satisfies their own sense of physical self and lets them feel discreet, allowing them to pass comfortably and safely.

As Milly's confidence in passing grew, she began to face the fact that she would have to, at some point very soon, come out at work, as a performer and as a teacher. Both avenues filled her with dread. In her own band, her colleagues were supportive but concerned that having a female guitar soloist would affect their fan base. Much of her other work was managed by an agency, for which she played as lead guitarist in several different covers bands. The agency dress code requirements were very specific, and there was an implicit assumption that all their guitarists were male. Milly was desperately worried that they would simply remove her from their roster for not meeting the 'look' and that she would sacrifice the major part of her income. Then there was her instrumental teaching for the local authority music department, where it was all too easy to imagine that parents and schools, whether through ignorance or bigotry, might not welcome a trans woman having one-to-one contact with their children. Nonetheless, the bullet had to be bitten. If Milly wanted the hormones and, in time, the surgery, the rules said that she had to have a full, documentable year of 'real life experience' in which she presented as a woman in all aspects of daily living. Until she announced herself in her professional life, that particular clock would not start ticking.

Once again, we sat at the kitchen table late into the night, staring down the facts and fears together. Confronting this final hurdle in her presentation had reduced Milly to a pale shadow of herself. 'I'm terrified,' she confessed. 'What if I lose all my work? I'm afraid of being laughed at and humiliated in schools. I don't know if people will be willing to book me for gigs any more. I don't know what the agency will let me wear, or if they'll even let me keep playing for them. I feel like I'm on the brink of abandoning everything I've worked for. But I've got to do it.' I knew that she was facing the prospect of losing the career that was at the core of her musical identity, and that this was the climax of a battle that had raged within her for years now. I was awestruck by her courage, and afraid for her too, though I tried not to let that show. Instead, I reassured her: 'If you feel that you have no choice but to transition – and you know that although I support you, I have my own fears and concerns about that – then you really have no choice but to take this risk. I can't see any other way forward. But, on the other hand, this is why we have anti-discrimination laws. It won't be easy, but I am sure the local authority will have policies in place and they will be legally obligated to protect you.'

'I don't know how to tell Pete,' she replied. Pete was her line manager, but outside Milly's workplace I also knew him personally in my own professional life as a fine violinist and decent person.

'You're lucky it's Pete. He'll be fine. I'm sure he will be kind and do everything he can to help you. I think if you don't know how to find the words, the best way would be to write to him.' I had a lightbulb moment. 'If you ask Pete to circulate the news on the last day of term, the rest of the staff won't have the opportunity to gossip about it. And by the time term starts again it will be old news.' In fact, I thought this was wildly optimistic, but I hoped it might ease Milly's anxiety a little. Shy at the best of times (except on stage), the thought of being the focus of office gossip was paralysing.

'What about Nick?' He was her agency manager, and from my point of view an unknown quantity. I had no idea if my advice was sound or not, but right now I felt Milly just needed someone to stand in her corner. Obviously, the job fell to me.

'Go and see him. You're their top guitarist. They won't want to lose you. If this "look" you're so worried about is such a big issue for them, go with some suggestions as to how you would like to dress and let them choose a new look that works for both of you. You need to talk to him. I don't think you can do this one by email,' I said.

'I'm terrified,' she said again.

'I know, but look how strong you've been all these years. You've survived worse. This is your moment to finally be true to yourself, to stand up and stop living a lie. Nothing could be braver, and I know that you can do it.' Behind my resolute facade I was crumbling. The look of anguish on my child's face tore up my heart. I still couldn't bring myself to even think about the physical aspects of what might lie ahead, but right now all I wanted to do, with every fibre of my being, was to stop that pain for her. If that meant claiming to have all the answers about how to navigate a successful gender transition in the music world, then I would be that person, though nothing was really further from the truth.

And so, the next afternoon, she grasped the nettle. Milly went to London to see Nick, and although he was, not surprisingly, taken aback, once they had talked strategy he was adamant that Milly would stay on board, fronting the agency's headline bands. Maybe, he mused, an agent to his bones, it could even be a selling point. It was agreed that she could adopt the dress code worn by their female singers, and, as easily as that, something which had seemed an impassable barrier was cleared. Her email to Pete had also been carefully drafted and dispatched, and it wasn't long before she received a warm and sympathetic response. Human Resources had dealt with this before, he said, sending through useful links to professional bodies, Musicians' Union LGBTQ reps and an occupational health helpline. At the end of term, Pete would inform the other instrumental teachers and brief the schools where she taught, and after the holiday Amelie would return to work as Miss.

In all of this, I think Milly was extremely lucky. The music business is by nature liberal and diverse, and as a professional environment it was probably the best possible place for Amelie to come out as trans. Elsewhere in the world of work, however, I now know that discrimination is rife and unemployment (and, consequently, homelessness and poverty) among trans people is endemic. Recent surveys have exposed that nearly half of all employers openly admit that they would not employ a trans person, and fewer than 5 per cent consider that a trans person would 'fit in' in their workplace. No wonder Milly was afraid. At least for me, ignorance had been bliss. Nonetheless, we both knew that it was almost certain that obstacles and humiliations lay ahead: at best misgendering, at worst abuse or even violence. But for the moment, Milly was riding high on adrenaline and all her feelings spilled out in a torrent of emotion. She cried and laughed, sweeping me up in her wake. I felt overwhelmed by the place where I now found myself, torn by conflicting feelings which I was not able to express. I shared Milly's joy as she finally leapt across the hurdle she had so greatly feared, but at the same time – and on this I could say nothing – for me, this was a defining moment too. The last vestige of my son had been erased, and now the progress could only be inexorably towards, well, I didn't know what. But in this it was Milly who mattered, not me, and it was Milly I needed to be here for. She trembled and sobbed with relief, daring at last to admit the dawn of hope for her future. Today was the real beginning. Today was the first official day of Amelie.

CHAPTER 8

With Amelie now fully fledged at home and at work, I really couldn't put off telling the rest of my family any longer. The gradual steps towards transition which Milly had taken had been easy to keep off the radar, and that had worked well for both of us as we found our feet in the new order of things. For my own sake especially I had kept a lid on the potential for added stress while Baz's life was hanging in the balance and Milly was in crisis, but now things were a little steadier I knew the time had come. My family is a very scattered lot, but even so we have remained close, often visiting each other and keeping in touch by Skype. Lucas and Serena were in Sydney, my brother Chris and his wife Clarissa were in Perth, my mother lived hundreds of miles south of them in the south-west corner of Western Australia, my sister Louisa and her husband James were in Melbourne and my father was in France. I was naturally concerned as to how they would all handle the news, not because I was worried (much) about upsetting them but because I didn't want to see Milly suffer the sting of misunderstanding or experience the pain of further rejection or ridicule. I hoped for the best, but knew I should at least be ready for the possibility of the worst.

I made the easiest call first. Chris and Clarissa have always been open-minded, intellectually curious and emotionally generous, and I knew Milly would have them on her side no matter what. They did not let me down, and their response was as understanding and supportive as I had hoped it might be. Of course, they expressed their great surprise and even greater concern, but they willingly and quickly shifted their perceptions and immediately welcomed the idea of their new niece, Amelie. I tried to gauge Chris's view on how our parents might respond. He thought, as I did, that although it was very probably not something our father had ever given thought to, he would accept it once he understood it. He might think it was weird, but he was unlikely to express any prejudice. Our mother, on the other hand, was notorious for wanting a picture-perfect family life (something I felt I had always failed her in) and a grandson who was really a granddaughter didn't sit easily in that silver frame. I doubted that she had ever heard of transgenderism, and I certainly knew it wouldn't be something she would be immediately comfortable with.

But she was nearly eighty and deserved a little leeway. I thought she'd come around. How my sister would take it was hard to guess, but she had always idolised Miles as a child so I thought she would probably be willing to accept it because of that treasured relationship. In any case, she was constantly travelling with work and so I would just have to get to her when I could.

Having analysed and ranked the prospects with Chris, I tackled my father down in Bordeaux next. As we talked, he struggled, as many people do, with a confusion between sexual orientation and gender identity. I tried to explain to him that the two are not connected and that, in a nutshell, sexual orientation is who you want to go to bed with, while gender identity is who you see yourself as when you do. The confusion is understandable, I suppose, if you are not well versed in all the available options. 'So, is he a transvestite, then?' he asked.

'Firstly, it's *she*, Dad, and secondly, no, she isn't a transvestite, as you call it. Being a cross-dresser is a fetish. Some people are emotionally or sexually fulfilled by wearing clothes belonging to the opposite gender, like a man wearing women's clothes for personal gratification. It's a way of dressing up, usually in private.' I really wasn't finding this new line of discussion a particularly easy one to address with my father but, as they say in France, once the wine is uncorked you have to drink it. 'Being transgender means that your inner sense of who you are as male or female doesn't match your biological body,' I went on. 'It's a completely different thing. It's not sexually exciting; it's an emotional necessity.'

After a short pause to process all this, he asked, 'So will he have his penis cut off, then?'

This really wasn't getting any easier. 'I don't know what lies ahead, Dad. She says she hopes to have sex reassignment surgery one day. But as far as I know, they don't actually... umm... cut the penis off. I think they kind of re-purpose it.' Actually I was pretty vague on the details myself and, to be honest, for now I preferred to keep it that way.

'Well, say hi to Miles from me. I'm sure it will all be fine.'

'Amelie, Dad,' I sighed. 'Amelie.' This was going to be a long road, but at least the signals from Bordeaux seemed to be positive. Mystified, but positive.

As it happened, I was due in Sydney in two weeks' time for work, so I decided I would delay telling Lucas and Serena until I could discuss it with them face to face. Some hurried diary coordination with my sister meant that we could also manage to meet for coffee and a chat while I was there. So, for now, that left my mother. I was nervous as I dialled her number. She adored both the children, but she was conservative and not widely experienced in the ways of the post-modern world. I just didn't know where to start. 'Mum,' I began tentatively, 'you know how Milly has been suffering from depression for so long? I think we might have finally got to the bottom of the problem. Miles has told me that the reason "he" was so unhappy is that she has always known that she was a girl. She has been depressed all her life from trying to cope with it all, but that's over now. She is transgender and has decided to come out as a trans woman and live her life as a female. From now on, her name is Amelie. She's changed it by deed poll and everyone knows at work. It's official. No more Miles. Milly is still fine, but her name is Amelie. You need to say she and her and hers when you talk to her from now on.'

My mother's voice quavered as she tried to find a way to reply that wouldn't offend or upset but would pour oil on these unwelcome troubled waters. She always liked to keep the peace, at whatever cost, in order to maintain the status quo. 'It's just a phase, darling. I don't think you need to make a big deal out of it.'

'No, Mum, it's definitely not just a phase. It's a lifetime of pain that has finally burst out into the open and it's time to fix it. She's Amelie, and I am supporting her as much as I possibly can.'

'I think she needs counselling. I've heard about these children who think they are what they're not. It's just silliness. They're pulled in by bad people and organisations and just want to be different. It's a fad. I'm sure you'll manage it beautifully and in a few months we'll be all back to normal.' One big, happy family.

'Mum, I've been dealing with this since last Christmas. I've spent months talking to Milly about it. She has to have counselling as part of the process anyway. It's not a fad. You are going to either have to get used to it or lose her. She will not stand for you calling her "he" or saying Miles. That life is dead to her now. I have a daughter and her name is Amelie. I know it seems harsh, but I'm saying this to help you. Either you accept it or you lose her. That's how serious it is.'

For once, my mother's interest in avoiding conflict paid dividends. She didn't want to lose me or Milly, as I knew she wouldn't, and so in effect she was aware that it was do or die. She decided to do. 'Alright, darling. I hear what you are saying. I will do my best. But I'll make lots of mistakes. I'm getting old; you can't ask too much of me. She'll always be my little Miles to me. Don't you remember Thomas and Buzz Lightyear?' Of course I did. I'd been there myself. Having a transgender child means turning yourself inside out and insisting that everyone you care about does the same. It's a path that can only be navigated by love. But fortunately, we had that. Whatever internal struggles my mother had with the concept, she still had the love to support the birth of my new daughter, and I knew that, however flawed, she would do her best to be there for both of us.

I was glad that my decision to tell Lucas and my sister when I was next in Sydney meant that I could now briefly pause in the task of revealing my daughter's extraordinary life change. This process wasn't just part of Milly's coming out; it was also my own coming out as the mother of a transgender child, and I was finding the experience quite draining. I had asked the others not to speak to Louisa until I had a chance to tell her myself. The matter was too sensitive to learn about at second hand, and in any case I wanted to make sure that things were portrayed accurately. I wasn't convinced that my parents' understanding currently stretched to that. The conversations had been difficult and stressful, but so far it had gone as well as I could have hoped, and for the most part their bewilderment was tempered by acceptance. I was grateful that at this point my family were on side and willing, albeit at a distance, to countenance the idea of Amelie. Rejection by family members is widespread among trans people, and a recent survey has revealed that around 57 per cent experience some kind of ostracism from their family. Some 40 per cent of the 6,500 trans men and women surveyed said that one or more relatives refuse to speak to or spend time with them because of their gender expression, and one in five have experienced domestic violence related to their transition. Milly, of course, had already been cast out by her own father, but I hoped that elsewhere the family would hold tight. I wasn't sure it would.

The imminent trip to Sydney was throwing up its own problems. Baz was stable at the moment but still needed constant monitoring and assistance, and I was deeply worried by the thought of being away for two weeks. Milly would be shouldering the burden of his care, and I felt horribly guilty having to ask her to do that. She had her own work and so was often on the road herself or gigging until the early hours. Lately, I'd had ad hoc carers helping out occasionally when Milly and I had a diary clash, but I couldn't rely on Bev and her girls for the night shift. Milly's bandmates, the two Ollies, Ollie Edwards and Ollie Dawson, came to the rescue. Metal heads they might be, but under the tattoos and piercings lurked big talents and hearts of gold. Without being asked, they offered to move in while I was away and share the responsibility for Baz's care with Milly. I couldn't have been more grateful.

I arrived in Sydney in the evening, shattered after more than twenty hours in the air and disorientated by the time difference. Lucas and Serena had made dinner, and once I'd washed away the grime of travel, we sat down to eat. If I'd been hoping for some relaxation at the end of a long journey and perhaps a little small talk over a glass of wine, I was quickly disabused of that idea. Lucas knew something was up and he was determined to get to the bottom of it. Now. 'Why are you being so cagey about Miles these days?' he asked. 'I know you've got a lot on your plate with Baz, but since that ridiculous outburst at Christmas Miles and Leigh have just shut down. We don't hear from them; you don't talk about them. What's going on?' Exhausted or not, it seemed I was going to have to tackle the matter head on.

'I've been waiting to see you until I told you this, but since that argument at Christmas Milly has told me that she is transgender. That is why she was so upset by some of the things that were said in that conversation.'

'What's the matter with you?' Lucas burst out. 'Why are you calling him "she"? Have you seriously drunk the Kool-Aid?'

'Milly has changed her name and her gender presentation. It's been a very difficult time, but she is now fully out and intends to live her life as a woman. I am supporting her, and I do call her "she". Quite apart from anything else, it's just respecting her wishes. Her name is now Amelie.'

Lucas was scornful and furious. 'So are you saying you actually think Miles is a female now? What do you mean by gender presentation? Don't tell me he's going around in a dress.'

I had no intention of getting drawn into this debate again. 'My only interest is in supporting Milly. And yes, she is now dressing as a woman.'

'So under that dress is a male pretending to be a woman, and you actually think that's OK?'

'She's not pretending. She truly believes that she is, and always has been, a girl. That she was born in the wrong body. It has caused her a lifetime of anguish, and finally she has taken the steps she feels she needs to take in order to be who she really is.'

'I asked you, "Do you think that's OK?"' Lucas repeated, his comment suffused with icy anger. 'Do you seriously believe that someone with XY chromosomes can just put on a dress and be a real woman? You're an intelligent person. Don't tell me you've been sucked into this nonsense.'

'My concern is only for Milly. I am giving you this news because you are Milly's brother. I hope you might think that she deserves your care and support too. She has suffered horribly in all sorts of ways and, for me, all that matters is keeping her safe and seeing her happy. I will leave the trans identity politics to others.' I was in an impossible situation, and my solution, craven though it was, was to avoid engaging. Amelie was my daughter, and my views on gender and genetics would remain for ever excluded from any discussion on that matter. What matters are compassion and the motivations of our heart. What matters are our souls and how we express them in this world.

* * *

My sister, Louisa, was the final piece of the jigsaw. I was still very bruised by Lucas's reception of the news and hoped this meeting might be easier. Louisa had always doted on Milly. We met in a Sydney café, all rough-hewn wood and industrial chic, with wildflower petals strewn artfully across the all-day breakfast, and half a dozen types of artisan coffee. I love eating in Sydney and it's my sister's line of work so it was easy to while away the time talking about the food and the ambience, and simply enjoying this rare chance to chat. But pleasant though it was, I couldn't avoid my reason for being there. I needed to put my anxieties aside and move on to the real point of our meeting.

'So,' I began cautiously, 'we haven't really talked about Milly yet.'

'I know!' Louisa said happily, spooning another mouthful of the ricotta hotcake with poached peaches. 'This is delicious. I love what they've done with the pistachio crumble. How is Miles? Guitar going well? Is he still with Leigh?'

'Well, that's the thing,' I said. 'Yes, the guitar's fine. Leigh's back in New Haven but they're still together. But Milly... well, things have changed a lot recently. Milly has come out as transgender.'

'What?' Louisa spluttered. 'You can't be serious. That's ridiculous. Miles has always been such a boy. What about the weight-lifting and the RAF?'

'That was all just an attempt to cope with the situation. You know that Milly has always suffered from depression. And now I know that this is why. For her whole life Milly has felt that she was really a girl. She's now officially transitioned and has changed her name to Amelie.'

'Surely you're not going along with this?'

'Of course I am. Milly is my child and I love her. And the difference in her now that she has transitioned is incredible. For the first time in her life she seems happy.'

'It's a fad, you know that.' Louisa looked angry and hurt. 'I've heard about it. All this transgender stuff in schools today. It gives them ideas, and the next thing, insecure and unhappy teenagers think they've got something that makes them different and interesting. It's attention-seeking, plain and simple. He needs a psychiatrist, not a personal stylist.'

And I needed another coffee. I had not expected Louisa to come down on this side of the equation.

'Believe me, Amelie does not need anything to make her different and interesting. Her music does that for her. This is something deep-rooted; it's fundamental. She is having counselling, because that is part of the process, but counselling certainly won't make her change her mind. I'm afraid the only mind that is going to need changing is yours. Either you accept her as she is or you lose your relationship with her. I'm not giving an ultimatum; I'm just explaining how it is.'

'I can't deal with this. I just don't believe it,' Louisa said, pushing her plate aside. 'You've had months to think about it, but for me it's a bombshell. I need time.' And so, on the steps of the café, surrounded by

Sydneysiders queuing for coffee and brownies from the street-side counter, we parted without words and she walked away, angry and distressed.

The tally was complete. Chris and Clarissa, a decisive yes. Mum, a reluctant yes. Dad, a bewildered yes. Lucas, no on principle (pending rational proof). Louisa, just no, or not yet. Welcome to the 57 per cent, Amelie. I'm sorry all your family couldn't be there for you. And here I am, stuck in the middle again. My children at odds, my sister dismayed and confused and two elderly parents floundering as they wrestled with what to say and how to understand this inexplicable turn of events. I dragged my way through the rest of the week, playing and teaching in a state of emotional exhaustion, but also finding some relief in that distraction. I was happy that I would soon leave all the swirling angst this bombshell had unleashed behind me. After my last class of the tour, I switched my mobile back on to find seventeen missed calls from Milly. Baz was refusing fluids and did not know who she was. He was confused and agitated. She had called a doctor. I needed to get home as quickly as I could.

CHAPTER 9

By the time I landed in London late the next day, Baz was in the grip of another virulent infection. The visiting locum had prescribed yet more antibiotics, but Baz's temperature had continued to climb and his delirium had worsened. Frightened by his hallucinations and uncontrollable shivering, Milly had called an ambulance, and when I arrived at the hospital directly from the airport I found her at his bedside with Edwards and Dawson. All three looked strained and exhausted. Baz was on intravenous antibiotics and fluids, and not making any sense at all. He was so weak he could barely talk, but in any case, anything he did say was sheer nonsense. I knew the score these days: his depleted white blood cell count made him susceptible to every kind of infection, and if it was a urinary tract infection that laid him low, delirium was usually its first indication. As dreadful as it was to see him in this condition, I actually felt rather relieved. I'd been through this before; I knew what the problem was, and how they would fix it. It would take a few days, but I felt reasonably confident that Baz would be home again soon, feeble certainly, but alive. In the meantime, I was spared having to tell Milly the news from Sydney, which I knew would devastate her, and cowardly though it was, I was glad about that. There was just too much else going on, and Baz's knife-edge condition gave me an excuse to avoid confronting her distress while I dealt with my own.

At the hospital, I was surprised to find Milly dressed in an even more feminine style than she had been daring a few weeks earlier when I left for Australia. Clearly, she was gaining confidence in her presentation now that she was fully out, and had begun, it seemed, to take further steps towards finding her own look. That look was unexpectedly girly. I had thought the androgynous rock style she had favoured was her natural self-expression, but to my amazement the unrelenting black of her previous clothes, all denims and leather, was replaced by colour, soft textures and figure-enhancing shapes. Truly a butterfly had unfurled from the chrysalis.

I have a treasured piece of jewellery, turquoise and deep-blue flower petals set in silver on a delicate chain, and I love to wear it in the summer. It has always brought me great pleasure; the colours are perfect and the little jewelled garland is delicate and pretty. Milly bought it for me with her pocket money from a craft fair when she was eight. She, my Amelie-that-was-Miles, had good taste even then, and I see it now as my daughter's first encounter with the outward signifiers of femininity and her wish to share that with me. I am reminded of Amelie's journey every time I wear it and I am saddened that it took so long for us to enjoy that together. But I could see that she had now found the courage to play with those early hidden desires. I was moved, but also fascinated and anxious in equal measure. It struck me, as I observed Milly's new style, that learning to look, walk and talk like a woman evolved out of a life experience of socialisation, nurtured by relationships with friends and role models. If you didn't have that experience, I supposed it might be difficult to achieve that effortlessly. Would someone who hadn't evolved through those awkward teenage years, trying on regrettable blue mascara and frosted eyeshadow in friends' bedrooms, pushing parental boundaries in 'don't you dare go out like that' outfits, have to live through similar ill-advised mistakes as an adult, until she found her style and acquired the necessary skills?

I wondered if that was why the trans women who are most visible in the media tended towards the stereotypical female extremes of the grooming spectrum. Why so many accessories? Why so much makeup? Why so hyper-feminine, sometimes to the point of caricature? Perhaps it is because they have never had the chance to experiment their way through those particular adolescent agonies (although I appreciate they had their own far more painful cross to bear) and therefore learnt their female craft largely from the gender stereotypes disseminated by film, magazines and, these days, Instagram. I think this is a much more complex issue than it first appears. Is it actually that trans women feel they need to frame themselves in superficially feminised ways in order to be 'believed'? If you have to constantly fight to prove that you are a woman, then perhaps the easiest way to do that is by resorting to stereotype, even if your best shot at 'passing' puts you in the firing line of ridicule. Or is it that in order to feel safe as a trans woman, for whom abuse and the fear of violence is an everyday reality, you need to make absolutely sure no one guesses you are trans? Either way, it is a horrible dilemma, and one I think that those who transition in middle age are most prone to.

The body is far more accepting of physical transition before the age of twenty-four, and those who can acquire hormones before this biological deadline have many advantages: clear skin, bright eyes, abundant hair, a slimmer and healthier physique. For people like Milly, the transition into trans womanhood was attainable within the parameters of our social ideals of beauty. But for the middle-aged trans woman going through transition, it is much, much harder. The body has broadened and the skin toughened, the hair is receding, the brow and jawline are more strongly masculinised. Thirty or forty years of testosterone does that to you. But my experience has taught me that trans women do not transition because they have a desire to adopt the trappings of femininity; they do so in the unshakeable knowledge that they are, at their core, female. Sometimes I like to wear overtly feminine clothes and enjoy the effect they have; at other times, I might be more comfortable in an old pair of jeans. Whichever I choose, I am always a woman. But I can easily understand that if my selfhood as a woman was likely to be mistaken or misinterpreted, I would make sure I was always wearing the dress or the heels, the lipstick or the bracelets, just so there could be no doubt in anyone's mind.

Although to my eye Milly seemed to be acquiring a very natural sense of style and was far from a parody, she nonetheless still lived in constant fear of not passing. Now that she had started to feel comfortable in her dress sense, she moved on to other details and, with the highly attuned ear of a musician, her greatest anxiety was for her voice. For most trans women, vocal presentation is one of the last elements to receive attention during transition, and many don't bother with it at all, but Milly's tenor voice caused her daily anguish. I now knew why she had spent the past ten years eyes down, mumbling into her long hair. Every word that came out of her mouth was a painful reminder that she was not who she felt she was. Milly was determined to transform the way she spoke and began to consider the possibility of professional vocal therapy. I had thought (if I had indeed thought about it) that sounding more like a woman would simply mean raising the pitch of the voice by adopting a kind of permanent falsetto, but as Milly started to talk to me about this aspect of her transformation, I realised that the reality is much more complicated.

Although for trans men simply taking testosterone is enough to lower the voice, the reverse is not true for trans women; oestrogen therapy has no effect on biologically male vocal cords, even if taken before puberty. A surgical procedure (cricothyroid approximation or CTA surgery) has been developed which sutures the vocal cords in tension to permanently raise the pitch of the voice. The shortcoming of this procedure, however, is that it *only* raises the pitch, and I was surprised to learn that that is not what makes a woman sound like a woman. Milly used the example of the satirical animated social comedy *South Park* to explain it to me. In *South Park*, the voice actors are adult males whose vocal pitch has been artificially raised by sound engineering software; the result is a voice that sounds childlike, not female. Women speak differently to men, not just in pitch but in resonance, intonation and style. And those traits are acquired by imitation and socialisation. Milly set about researching the subject with her usual rigour and, after reading everything she could find on the subject, she settled on a shortlist of therapists, finally deciding on a vocal coach in London who specialised in helping trans women find their voice.

Kristina's consulting rooms were in Harley Street, the world-famous medical enclave in London, where stuccoed Georgian frontages have housed discreetly prestigious private healthcare since the nineteenth century; a place where the cost of treatment is proportional to the value of the real estate. Milly was willing to throw everything she had at this new endeavour, and she was excited and optimistic as she set off to Harley Street for her first appointment. Over the next three months, Milly travelled to London every week for vocal coaching with Kristina. At each session, she was given exercises to practise, and if there was one thing Milly knew how to do, it was practise. She approached her vocal exercises with the same unwavering dedication that she brought to her guitar technique schedule. Kristina's worksheets were timetabled alongside all the scales and arpeggios, finger exercises and picking styles that formed the cornerstone of Milly's daily routine. She would wander around the house intoning, 'Move more. Meet me. My mind. Most merry,' and so on (and on) for hours at a time.

The first building block of feminising the voice is not just raising its pitch but, more crucially, changing its resonance. Male voices resonate in the chest, but female voices resonate in the head. The 'm' sounds of moving more and making merry worked on shifting this resonance into the larynx and sinuses. They had to be repeated endlessly until that shift became the natural location of the voice. I was intrigued and, to be honest, quietly amused by this mysteriously beautiful long-legged girl in my kitchen, murmuring 'my mind most merry meet me make me move more' under her breath as she made cups of tea and ate peanut butter out of the jar. If I found it gently funny, Milly certainly didn't. One day, loitering in the kitchen, chatting as I cooked, I laughed out loud, tickled with momentary amusement as Milly moved and met and minded yet again. Milly exploded with anger at what to her was thoughtless cruelty and ran furiously from the room, crying with hurt at my perceived mockery. It seemed to me that every step of this journey was fraught with elephant traps, and try as I might to be supportive, it was so easy to make a mistake that would reduce my daughter to anguish all over again. Despite my best efforts I all too often put my foot wrong, but I know that the deep pain of traversing life as a trans person requires and deserves fathomless levels of sensitivity from those around who love and care.

Once Milly had learnt to shift the resonance of her voice, she began to work on breath control and air speed. In the mystifying transgender world in which I found myself, at last here was a topic on which I could claim some expertise. As a flute player, these were concepts I understood well. I was completely fascinated by the process of Milly's vocal feminisation, and by the change I could hear week on week in her voice. She had now moved on to vowel sounds and the letter 'h', both of which required a different way, as a woman, of using the air column and the soft palate. In flute playing, I had always thought it was the aspiration of the vowel and not the articulation of the consonant that carried the sound, and I was rather pleased to have my theory confirmed by a Harley Street speech specialist. 'How happy. Her hair. Hold hands. High hopes,' went the new practice routine. 'In Hertford, Hereford and Hampshire, hurricanes hardly happen.' It was as if Eliza Doolittle had taken up residence in my studio and was trying her hardest to meet the exacting demands of Professor Higgins's elocution instruction (though having learnt my lesson previously, I made sure that particular thought did not escape into the open). Milly's modulation and phrasing were also beginning to alter, and again as a musician this was something I understood. Shaping a phrase is the very essence of its expression, and so it made sense to me that this was a vital part of the transformation.

Real change set in at around four weeks, and after twelve weeks of therapy and practice Milly had completely changed her voice. It was breathier, gentler, higher, more melodic. She spoke a little faster, and had learnt to use different kinds of expression (phatic utterances, as they are called; words such as 'umm', 'like' or 'alright?', which mean little but fill the gaps in conversation) that are typical of the way women are socialised to speak. Men apparently have quite different modes of expression, which I suppose we are so used to that we don't notice until it is pointed out. All this rather unsettled me, not because I was uncomfortable with Milly's voice but because it made me think about my own. Where was I on this spectrum? I had been fascinated to read that vocal pitch in women varied according to their level of education, with more highly educated women adopting a lower tone, and I suspected this was true of me. I find a high-pitched, girly voice quite grating, and probably give it less intellectual credence. Did I need to examine my prejudices? I was also ashamed to find that I actively disliked this new, breathier tone that Milly was acquiring. Why, I thought, should being a woman mean sounding feeble? I wanted my daughter to take my example of what I hoped was a resilient and fearless kind of womanhood. This meant a lot to me, having been hard won through those early years of unhappiness and struggle. I wanted to model for her a woman who could stand up, hold firm, achieve her goals, reach the top shelf. Someone who knew how to love and how to be passionately, tenderly female but who also knew how to survive. I realise now that these concerns were just part of the learning process for both of us. The exaggerated femininity of Milly's voice has moderated and now that it has settled I can no longer call to mind how she sounded before her transition. And as far as inner resolve goes, I hadn't even begun to see the iron that lay at her core. Those days were still ahead.

In the meantime, Baz was a constant concern, and Milly and I were as desperate as ever as we juggled the needs and stress of his care. He ebbed and flowed in lucidity and strength, but day by day the thread attaching him to this world seemed ever more tenuous. He slept a great deal, and that was a relief, as it allowed me to get some work and practice done. It reminded me of the baby years when I could collapse in a combination of guilt and joy as my infant quieted to the world. In the same way, though, sometimes the dark hours seemed unending. There was no real distinction between night and day, and I could as easily find myself negotiating Baz's insistent intention to head off to London at two in the morning as trying to rouse him to take fluids or medicine at midday. Work was the one unvarying undercurrent of this never-ending crisis, and both Milly and I were caught up in the freelance musician's erratic life of rehearsals, gigs, teaching, admin and project planning. Having Milly living at home was not just a way of helping her get established financially and find her feet through her transition; for me, it was a collaboration that ensured our mutual survival.

We supported each other, and I think it was the understanding that came from living through the same unusual professional stresses that kept us afloat as we juggled work, care and the demands of various relationships. It wasn't easy, though, and life veered precipitously between responsibility and comedy. Black concert dress of one sort or another was always draped from the clothesline, though, needless to say, Milly's was rather cooler than mine – still, I had offered to share if she wanted to experiment. Tonight, though, a carer was coming to watch over Baz, and Milly and I both had concerts. I had ironed my black chiffon blouse and taken out my softly pleated black silk skirt earlier in the day and they were hanging in the wardrobe ready for the show that night. Worrying about my concert dress was very much secondary to anxieties about the evening's performance, but when I went to pack my bag I couldn't seem to lay my hands on that blouse. I put it down to stress. Or Baz, I supposed. He often did bizarre and erratic things these days. It didn't matter, I had a rail full of black clothes and an alternative was quickly and easily packed in the case. I needed to get a grip, I told myself. I got home late that night and was winding down with a quiet glass of post-concert wine when Milly walked in an hour or so after me. She looked so beautiful in that delicate chiffon blouse. Probably much better than I ever did.

CHAPTER 10

If I made frequent small mistakes, like tactlessly laughing at a voice exercise, or bigger ones, like accidentally misgendering my daughter, I was also at times guilty of other, far worse errors. In trying to write about my own journey as the mother of a transgender child as honestly as I can, I have to admit to these mistakes, though I would much rather publicly congratulate myself on my impressive sensitivity and compassion and tell my story of Milly's coming out and transition in a self-satisfied rainbow-coloured halo. I always tried my hardest, with no other roadmap than love for my child, but I cannot ignore the times when I did fail to understand exactly what Amelie was experiencing, or through ignorance somehow found myself perilously close to bigotry (as I have been reminded many times). I think it's fair to say I've got much better at it, but our journey has been an immense learning curve for me and, having walked this path, I don't think there's any shame in that. As with any new learning, there will inevitably be times when we get it wrong, and for those times when I did, I hope I can be forgiven (and I think I mostly have been). I went to my first Pride event not that long ago to see Milly perform, and I had a blast. These days, I really do know what it means to be out and proud.

My first response when Milly came out to me that dreadful Christmas was to ask her to agree to have counselling before she went any further. I didn't say she was wrong, or that I didn't believe her, but I did feel it was vital that she really examined what she was contemplating. I even offered to pay. There are two things I realise now: firstly, counselling for gender identity issues will never make someone with genuine gender dysphoria say, 'Ah, yes, actually I probably was just acting out some other deeper problems. You've helped me realise I was wrong. I'm over it.' And secondly, by offering to pay, it seemed to Milly that this was exactly the outcome I was hoping for. She agreed, I think to keep me on side, but at the time she was very hurt. On this, at least, I think my conscience is clear. I truly just wanted my new daughter to make sure she had worked through the many complex issues she had experienced during her childhood and teenage years before adding something else so fundamentally life-changing. It was obvious to me that, at the bare minimum, a troubled relationship with her father and an unhappy boarding school experience would have played a significant and damaging part in her life. If I then added into the mix the grief she was experiencing as we watched Baz dying before our eyes, and the huge burden of responsibility for his care that she was sharing with me, counselling seemed reasonable, at least to me. In my defence, although I was not trying to change her mind about being transgender, I did think it would be worthwhile unpicking all these strands before she made any decisions. But I accept that, good though my intentions had been, this was the wrong thing to say and, understandably, left Milly feeling angry and unheard. When someone finally bares a deep, transgressive secret to you, suggesting that the first thing they need is a therapist is, at best, tactless, and not surprisingly open to misinterpretation. As I say, I've learnt a lot.

Nonetheless, I was actually right about the need for therapy. Milly did need counselling, but that was because it is an essential requirement of the gender reassignment process. There are strict international protocols for gender-affirming medication and surgery, and psychotherapy is the first step. A letter from a therapist confirming the patient's absolute commitment to their gender identity is needed in order to start on hormone therapy (two letters from different therapists if taking the NHS route) and, much later in the process, two psychiatric assessments also have to be produced before any surgery can be agreed. After some research and a few unsatisfactory trial sessions with various practitioners, Milly found someone she felt she could work with. Her new therapist, Susie, was not a specialist in 'gender affirmation counselling', and again, in my ignorance, I thought this was a good thing. If one believed everything one heard and read, these gender-affirming types were a scourge on confused teens and desperate young adults. I wanted Milly to talk things through with someone who was a neutral listening ear; someone who could give her insight and support without judgement one way or the other.

I know now that gender identity counselling explores a patient's gender history from a starting point of under-standing their personal development and the impact of life events. Until these have been addressed, a good therapist will not even begin to discuss transgender identity management and gender expression. The idea that a qualified specialist therapist could lead a patient into confirming mistaken beliefs about their gender identity is nothing short of offensive, and although the therapist will listen and provide professional assistance, the patient alone is fully responsible for those decisions and outcomes. In any case, Milly knew absolutely who she was, and she used the sessions with Susie to talk about the issues that had also concerned me (her father, school, Baz, as well as other things which are none of my business). Of course, her transgender identity was part of that mix, but other matters took precedence, and after a few months the sessions drew to a natural close. Susie provided the vital letter that would enable Milly to begin hormone therapy, and the counselling only confirmed her absolute need to transition.

I too was having counselling. Baz's terminal illness and the harrowing psychosis that went with it, Milly's transition and her emotional volatility, my attempts to repair the schism in our wider family and my fading hopes for a reconciliation, and the need to keep my professional life alive through all of this without losing my head was taking a considerable toll on me. I was exhausted and on edge almost all the time, and a full night's sleep was a rare blessing. Travelling for work was my one relief, and going to France, as I did frequently, restored my soul. I loved the culture, the history, the landscape, the language, the food and the wine. France was my touchstone. Every time I did go away for concerts and courses, though, I was aware that I was simply transferring the burden onto Milly, and that guilt pursued me mercilessly. Unlike Milly, I didn't find my own counselling terribly helpful. I had been referred by my doctor to a cognitive behavioural therapist, this being the type of therapy most readily available, but I wasn't feeling engaged with it.

Cognitive behavioural therapy is very strategy-focused, breaking down problems into smaller parts to arrive at solutions and resolutions, and is generally (at least when budget is a consideration) popular for its quick-fix approach. To me, though, it all felt a bit pointless. By nature I tend to be a very analytical thinker anyway and find it quite easy to grasp the overview of a situation quickly. I make my plans accordingly, no matter what the situation, so I didn't particularly appreciate a therapist trying to lead me towards 'action ideas'. I already had plenty of ideas and plenty of action. If anything, I found my therapist's apparently awestruck and even prurient admiration of my transgender experiences annoying. I felt that I didn't deserve her praise and, of everything that currently beset me, this was where I was most at sea. I didn't need counselling because I couldn't work out how to manage my life; I needed counselling because I was attempting to stay afloat in a perilous undertow of stress and emotional confusion. I was irrationally angry with Baz, blindsided by the toll his illness had taken on my life and loathing the saintly aura I felt I had to wear as his carer. It helped to talk about that, of course, and to be reassured that these feelings were quite normal, but I still felt I was floundering with Milly.

So far, I'd tried to do as much as I possibly could to help her, and I thought she was happy enough with that support (on the whole), but I now needed to confront some of the really big issues, ones I was grappling with now and ones I knew lurked around the corner. I no longer felt bereaved of a son, but I had not yet settled into unfailingly seeing my child as my daughter. At times, when I was caught short by that disjunct, I felt disappointed with myself for feeling that way, when I knew how great Amelie's own suffering was. And sometimes, I felt angry for failing to glide through these monumental changes without putting a foot wrong. I liked to get things right and always tried to tackle whatever I was engaged with to the very best of my ability, but in these uncharted waters I wasn't confident that I was or even could. As for thinking about the treatments that lay ahead, I knew that hormones would be next, but then what? Surgery, I supposed, and that idea I couldn't even begin to contemplate. Equally, the idea of coping with Baz's death, which I knew all too well was coming soon, left me wanting nothing more than to cover my head with my pillow and hide until the world had somehow sorted itself out.

The counselling left us both rather fragile, and I noticed that Milly had started to become agitated by what she felt was a lack of progress in her transition. Having finally faced the emotional risk of coming out fully, and made great strides through the anxiety-ridden process of beginning to dress and speak like a woman, Milly had reached a plateau. She was distressed at the idea that she had, for the moment, stalled. Although many trans women are happy to adopt only certain outward elements of transition, this was far from the case for Amelie. For her, nothing less than a complete bodily transformation would give her the peace and sense of rightness she longed for. Milly had not paused her transition during the months of counselling. She knew unequivocally that no matter what she confronted during those sessions, nothing would change her inner sense of who she was. So, alongside the therapy she had begun to take another cosmetic step towards physical change.

Milly was now well advanced in a programme of laser hair removal which she hoped would, once completed, leave her entirely free of facial hair. Her beard, light though it was, was a curse to her. She despised every last hair of it and shaved obsessively, often several times a day. The bathroom was overflowing with shaving supplies – razors, sharper razors, super-sharp razors, and a constantly changing array of brushes, gels, foams and balms – which she hoped might have a magical beard-annihilating effect. If she saw the faintest whisper of a shadow, even one that could be covered with makeup, she would often refuse to go out of the house, or, if she had no choice, she would leave miserably for work, swathed in scarves and hats in a desperate attempt to disguise the disgusting appearance that existed in her imagination. It was easy to understand why such an obvious and visible signifier of male physiology was abhorrent to her, so I was happy that at least she had some power of action in this aspect of her transition. So much else seemed blocked by the slowly grinding wheels of the healthcare system.

Milly was fortunate that her hair colouring meant

that laser hair removal would, to a certain extent, work for her, but she also expected to need facial electrolysis to make the result absolute and permanent. In cosmetic laser therapy, a pulse of light is transmitted into the hair follicle to destroy it. The process is only effective on dark hair (fair, white or grey hair does not absorb the light pulses, which I imagine is yet another difficulty for people transitioning later in life) and it only works at certain stages of hair follicle growth, which means repeated treatment is required. The laser moves step by step, repeatedly targeting areas the size of a small coin, and the pain, Milly told me, is like being repeatedly stung and flicked by a red-hot elastic band; tolerable, but only just. The electrolysis, on the other hand, she found almost unbearable. For Milly, this was a small price to pay for a solution to her problem.

Eight sessions of laser treatment were followed by more than twenty hours of electrolysis in torturously painful two-hour sessions, but eventually Milly was virtually hair free on her face, and she was thrilled with the result. At last, she had annihilated that particularly repellent marker of her past self. I knew, though, that epilation of the facial hair was only the beginning of the hair removal process. Milly had little in the way of chest and other body hair, and what she did have she dealt with by waxing, but soon her pubic hair would also have to go. Removing the pubic hair around the perineal and scrotal area was not only an aesthetic choice; it was a

clinical one. If she was to have sex reassignment surgery in due course, this hair had to be completely and
permanently removed. Some surgeons simply cauterise
the hair on the scrotum before surgery, but this is not
failsafe and can result in internal hair growth at a later
stage, so full pre-surgical epilation was Milly's chosen
option. The spacing of laser sessions, which had to be
six weeks apart because of the hair follicle lifecycle,
meant that long-range planning was required to reach
the end goal at the right time; however, this had the
advantage that it would also allow Milly time to save up
for yet another financially crippling treatment.

As with everything that mattered to Milly, she applied an utterly single-minded determination to the
project. Having decided on full epilation, she wanted to
make progress with the pubic hair as soon as she could
and so was seduced by a cosmetic clinic advertisement
for an interest-free credit deal that would let her pay
the thousands of pounds over time. I was not reassured
by the credentials of the clinic, nor by their reviews, and
was upset when I discovered that she had been lured in
by a 'pay £800 now, get £1,200 of treatment on credit'
deal. The salon staked out their niche by claiming to be
specialists in treating trans women, which I realise now
is just code for being willing to treat pre-operative trans
women at all. Many others refuse to. But I just didn't
like the look of this outfit; it was superficially glossy and
highly commercial, but therapeutic information and

testimonials were thin on the ground. As it turned out, my judgement was right.

Milly was relaxed as she headed off to her first appointment, expecting to need nothing more than a few painkillers to see her through the session, but a couple of hours later she was home again, doubled over with agony. Instead of starting with a consultation and a patch test, the practitioner had gone straight to work without even pausing to adjust the wavelength of the light to suit Milly's skin type and hair colour. After an hour of terrifying pain, her entire genital area had been severely burnt by the laser. Milly was incoherent with shock when she walked in the door, shaking and crying. It took five minutes to get any kind of sense out of her, but as she began to explain what had happened I was consumed by fury. Her skin, she told me, was purple and black. My daughter had already suffered so much in the process of her transition that to see her physically damaged by this charlatan, who took £800 of her hard-earned money in advance for his efforts, outraged me. I helped Milly upstairs so that she could lie down, brought her an ice pack and the strongest painkillers I could find. What did they think they were doing? How dare they damage my already damaged, beautiful daughter? Anger made me near irrational. I wanted to go in fighting, to pour all my maternal anguish on them and somehow make it right, but I knew that Milly was an adult and had to address this herself. I couldn't argue about credit agreements on her behalf or berate technicians I hadn't met. Milly would have to take action against them once she had recovered from her injuries and breathless agony. With her usual determination, though, she did just that and fought hard for justice. Eventually, she did get every penny of her £800 back and the credit agreement torn up, but the physical and emotional scars lasted a long time. Yet again, I was awed by her dignity, persistence and unshakeable sense of who she was and where she needed to go.

It took around eighteen months in total to complete Operation Epilation. Eight of the electrolysis sessions were covered by the healthcare system, which recognises that facial hair is a cause of significant mental health problems in trans patients, but eight sessions is not enough for anyone to achieve complete removal of facial hair, and so, although better than nothing, it is only really a top-up for self-funded treatment. The end cost was high in every way. Milly stoically endured hours of excruciating pain and she would often come home from the sessions trembling and mute. But for Milly it was worth every minute of suffering. Once the process was finished, she was overjoyed that she was no longer in a mental and practical battle with her facial hair, and she shone with a new kind of self-esteem.

The removal of her pubic hair was another milestone: a tangible sign that she was moving forward towards the sex reassignment surgery that was her unwavering goal. Although there was not the slightest indication as to when that might eventually happen, Milly did at last feel she was on her way. As I watched Amelie gain in confidence and inner beauty through all these stages, I was reminded of a famous quote by the great renaissance sculptor Michelangelo. 'The sculpture is already complete within the marble block before I start my work,' he said. 'It is already there, I just have to chisel away the superfluous material.' Amelie was chiselling away the superfluous material of the stone-hard mantle of her former being, and I found it fascinating to watch how every step of this journey was gradually uncovering the real person within, giving birth to that new life in an act of self-affirming creation.

CHAPTER 11

Baz died on a bright spring morning just before Easter, when the magnolia was in blossom and the snowdrops and crocuses were fading. Soon a wash of yellow would spread along the village roadside as the daffodils took their turn to bloom, but this year he would not see them. It was finished, and I was glad. His passing had not been beautiful or peaceful. There had been no tender deathbed words, no gentle pressing of hands or meaningful looks; just the harsh reality of a rasping, gasping, failing body shutting down to the world, a mind now gone to those around who had cared and loved. I was stunned by the horror of the experience, and the only emotion I could summon as I stumbled out of the hospital into the daylight was relief that it was finally over. Grief would come later, surging in waves when least expected, but at that moment I was in a daze, simply focused on surviving.

The beginning of the end had started three weeks earlier. Baz had been in a nursing home since November, when his deteriorating condition meant that his care had finally become more than any of us could manage, but he was as stable as he could have been in the circumstances. Milly or I, or both of us, visited him at least twice a day, and I had no particular cause for concern when I set off to London that morning for a day of rehearsals and meetings. My phone was off, as it had to be, so it wasn't until I switched it on again after work that I discovered a flood of texts and missed calls from Milly. My heart plunged at the news. Baz had been taken to hospital by ambulance. She didn't know why. The messages were confusing and when I managed to get hold of her Milly seemed unsure about what had happened. The nursing home had rung her and told her that he'd been taken to hospital; they didn't say which one but they said that they'd photographed the injuries. What injuries? She didn't know. I was bewildered and horrified. I hadn't been expecting this. Another infection, yes, but injuries? Why no further information? Where was he? A phone call to the nursing home gave me little more detail; they didn't know which hospital the ambulance had taken him to, and their only interest seemed to lie in covering their own backs as they carefully assured me they had filled out an accident report form and taken photos. I didn't waste any further time talking to them. That could wait.

Logical deduction told me he must be at Addenbrooke's Hospital, as it was the nearest one with an emergency room. Milly could get there much faster than I could, so I sent her to look for him while I raced across London to King's Cross for a train back to Cambridge. By the time I picked up my car and drove away from the station, a couple of hours had already passed. I found Milly at Baz's side in a cubicle curtained off from the general mayhem of A&E. Once again Baz was incoherent and hallucinating, but now also clearly in extreme pain. 'He's just come back from X-ray,' Milly told me. 'They say he's broken his hip.' I was appalled. How could this have happened? Baz was extremely frail and was meant to be under close supervision in the nursing home. Sitting by his bedside, we seemed to wait endlessly for information as different medical staff came and went, but slowly I pieced the story together. Baz had come down with a mild cough during the morning, which had developed rapidly into a dangerous fever. Why had the nursing home not called me or Milly? More importantly, why had the nursing home not called a doctor or given him his stand-by antibiotics? Baz's temperature spiked at thirty-nine degrees and in a state of febrile confusion he managed to get out of bed and struggle down the hallway of the home, where he fell and broke his hip. But at least they photographed the injury. They photographed a desperately ill, injured man sprawled lost and weeping on the floor before they moved to help him or call an ambulance. I have that photo, and I will never forgive them for it.

It was three in the morning by the time an orthopaedic registrar arrived to see me. 'We will need to do a hip replacement,' he said. 'He'll go to surgery in the morning and then he'll be on the ward for a few days for some rehabilitation. Should be home right as rain after that.'

'I don't think you have a full picture of what's going on here,' I replied. 'Firstly, he's no longer at home. He's in a nursing home that has proved itself to be utterly negligent in his care, and under no circumstances will he be going back there. Secondly, he is terminally ill, and even before this happened things were not looking good. He has aggressive myelodysplasia with refractory cytopenia and Lewy body disease. As well as a chest infection. Surely surgery is too much of a risk when he is this weak?' Myelodysplasia is a rare kind of blood cancer and my recently acquired medical fluency was largely courtesy of Google.

'Even if we think someone is likely to die soon we will do the replacement,' the register said. 'If he survives it will make him more comfortable, if nothing else.'

'But what about his haematology? He has almost no platelets; his blood won't clot. His white blood cells are failing, and the red ones aren't great either. How can you operate?'

'I haven't seen his full medical notes. I didn't know

about that.' How was this even possible? Baz had me there to fight for him and I was well informed about his condition. I was not afraid to stand up to doctors if I thought they were wrong, but it made me angry to think that other vulnerable patients might not have someone there to advocate for them in the same way. 'That's good to know,' the registrar said. 'I'll get the duty haematologist over to see him.'

The haematologist was nearing the end of her shift at another hospital several miles away, and so another hour went by without any progress. At least Baz had been knocked out by the strongest pain medication they could throw at him, and I sat by his bed in the noisy ward, grimacing my way through a hot drink from the vending machine (it claimed to be coffee, but I had my doubts) and occasionally allowing myself to doze. It seemed a long time since I'd set off to London that morning, full of musical thoughts and looking forward to a day with colleagues. I'd sent Milly home to sleep. There was no point both of us being wiped out. In the meantime, Baz's notes had been hurriedly retrieved from the oncology department, and his latest discouraging blood count was waiting for the haematologist when she finally arrived. 'We can transfuse him with platelets before the surgery,' she said, 'and then he'll need more transfusions afterwards. It's not an ideal scenario, but it's doable. I'll order up the platelets now and they'll be able to operate in a few hours' time.' I signed the authorisation for surgery, seeing no other alternative, and kept my vigil until Baz was finally wheeled away. I was not sure if I would see him again, and tears ran down my face as I quietly said goodbye and, in my head, made a little prayer for his safe return. If I'd known what was to come, I probably would have skipped that bit.

In the remains of that night, which was quickly turning into morning, I managed a few hours of fitful sleep before I returned to the hospital. Baz was out of post-operative recovery, alive, and back on a ward. I found him awake but barely lucid. Tubes curled around him like spaghetti; bloods in, wound drains out, fluids in, catheter out. He was a shell of himself, lying rigid in his ill-fitting hospital pyjamas and dressings and groaning quietly in pain. I was appalled all over again. By the second day, Baz was slightly more alert, and ward physiotherapists came to mobilise him. It was agony and, although they told me it was the standard procedure after a hip replacement, I felt helpless and angry seeing him forced to attempt these tiny movements. His suffering was unbearable to watch. Baz was hardly able to talk but I could read his eyes and knew that he could not take any more either. From that day, he began to refuse food. I would try to spoon tiny slivers into his mouth, a few crumbs or a half-teaspoon of soup, but soon he rejected even that and a speech therapist was called to the ward. With Baz's speech therapist there was no 'move more' or 'high hopes' to be heard; instead, this one was here to assess whether the feeding problem lay with Baz's swallowing reflex. It did. Baz had lost the ability to swallow and now the slightest misplaced morsel could choke him. It was not something that he would recover. Feeding became even more difficult. Food had to be liquidised and then a powder was added to turn it into a kind of gel. Even water had to be jellied and taken in fairy-sized spoonfuls. Anyone, I thought, would lose the will to live if that was their gastronomic outlook.

I cleared my diary, giving away whatever work lay ahead over the next few weeks to colleagues who were kind enough to cover for me. Life revolved around the hospital ward, where Milly and I took turns to sit with Baz, occasionally attempting to encourage him to take some sustenance. The orthopaedic registrar's jovial assurance that Baz would be home right as rain in a couple of days was a bitter joke. Instead, every day Baz was visibly losing strength. He had now not eaten for ten days, and I found myself on my phone desperately researching questions like 'How many days does it take to starve to death?' (answer: you die of dehydration first). His body was a barely fleshed skeleton and it was obvious to me that he was dying, so when a rattling cough was diagnosed as pneumonia I knew I needed to make a stand on his treatment. Surely, I thought, it was better to let this weary soul depart in peace, to let this body relieve itself of a world that it no longer needed or wanted. It was time for me to have the courage to say farewell in strength and sorrow rather than to take advantage of medical science to extend his suffering for the sake of a few more days or weeks. I begged the doctors to withhold the antibiotics for the pneumonia and signed a 'Do Not Resuscitate' form, but, nonetheless, the medical battle continued. Every time I went home for some sleep, or a shift changed over, it seemed that my request to allow Baz to pass away peacefully when the time came was ignored anew. Not one of the staff that passed like ships in the night through the ward was prepared to take responsibility for an action that might ultimately cause the death of a patient on their watch. Sadly, the fear of litigation apparently triumphs over both sense and humanity.

I reached breaking point one morning a few days later, when I arrived back on the ward after a few hours' sleep to find Baz yet again on intravenous antibiotics. 'Why?' I shouted at the nurses' station. 'Why? Please tell me why. Can't you see he's dying? Why are you doing this to him? He can't eat, he can hardly speak, he can't move without pain, he's nothing but bones. What are you hoping to gain by this?' I was crying inconsolably, and a kindly nurse took me to a private room. She listened to me – for the first time I felt someone really listened to me – as I explained what had been happening day after day. 'Don't you think he is dying?' I asked.

'Yes, he is dying,' she replied gently. It was the first time anyone had dared to confirm what I already knew. It gave me the courage to go on.

'How long do you think he might live? His quality of life is gone. It's obvious there's no hope. It's killing me, it's killing my daughter, it's killing all of us.'

'It's never an easy question to answer. But I would say a few more days at the most. We've been giving him fluids, which means he could last around three weeks without food. It's already been two weeks, so it won't be long. Most people don't want to know,' she added. 'They just want to keep trying.'

'I'm not most people.' I said. 'I don't want to be responsible for taking his life. Of course I don't. But I don't want him to suffer any more than he has to, and I can see that he is suffering every day. I can see that, really, he's already gone. It's time.'

'What do you want us to do?' the nurse asked quietly.

'Don't give him antibiotics for the pneumonia. Don't treat him for anything now. Just give him fluids and pain relief. I will stay with him as much as I can, but if things change when I am not here, call any time of the day or night and I will come straight away.'

'I will make sure everyone knows and I will make sure that it is part of every shift handover,' she promised. I left the room shaken but calm. It was painful, but

I believed her and trusted now that the end would be allowed to come in its time. None of us can hide from that truth and there is peace in accepting it.

The call came a few days later. Baz's breathing was becoming irregular, his body temperature was falling and he was being kept comfortable with a forced-air warming blanket. I should come now; it wouldn't be long. I left immediately for the hospital, phoning family and close friends as I drove. Milly would meet me there, and my mother was making arrangements to fly over as soon as she could get on a plane. In the end, though, it took much longer than any of us expected. Milly and I sat by Baz's bedside almost constantly for three days and nights. His breath rattled in his chest and came and went in rasping, arhythmic wheezes. His hand was cool and papery to the touch, and his eyes seemed to bulge from his emaciated skull. They were filmy and yellow, rimmed with red, unseeing. Occasionally he would reach forward and then fall back again, and sometimes a movement that might perhaps have been a smile passed momentarily across his face. Milly asked for time alone with Baz, and she sat and spoke to him, beset by silent grief. I had my private hours too, and I used them to say everything that needed to be said. I spoke with deep honesty about life and about love, of hopes and of the future, of sorrow and of gratitude. I hoped that he heard me and, though it was painful, there was a sense of completion.

Baz's body became restless and jerky, and the nurse suggested that subcutaneous morphine would ease his rigours. I held his hand as she administered the quieting medication, and his breathing, though sparing and irregular, became a little gentler. Suddenly, to my surprise and pleasure, it seemed that he was trying to speak to me, and I waited intently for his final treasured words. 'Ha… ha…', he gasped. 'Ha… have I given you my business card?' There is no romance in death, only absence and change, and the realisation that we should not waste a single precious moment or gift that life offers us.

I left the hospital alone, Baz's meagre effects in a green plastic hospital carry bag, and stumbled out into that spring sunshine. It was over, and what now? I did what I always did when I needed space just to be. I went to my special place, a favourite woodland deep in the Cambridgeshire countryside, and there I walked and walked for hours. I shouted at the world and shook my fist at the sky. I curled up under an ancient oak tree where I wept for all the pain and suffering and for what was no more. And then I went home and did what you have to do when someone dies, which is phone all the people waiting to hear the news, and send out dozens of texts, and open the cupboards full of a dead man's clothes and slam them shut again and say not now, not now. Milly and I got a takeaway that night, curry I think, but I couldn't really eat it. Tomorrow there were death certificates and cremation forms to sign, a funeral to organise and brain stem and spinal cord donation agreements to deal with. If I could spare someone else going through what we'd all suffered by donating Baz's tissue for research, I wanted to do that. And then I slept until the sun was high in the new day's sky.

CHAPTER 12

The funeral was two weeks later in a church that has stood for seven centuries on a gentle rise at the edge of the village. Well-meaning suggestions that mourners should wear brightly coloured clothes or that Baz's life might be celebrated with favourite tunes and a slide show rang hollow for me. Everyone has their own path through grief, and I needed to mark this passing with solemnity. My way of controlling the emotional turmoil that had engulfed me was by returning to the Church of England's unchanging ritual and the matchless poetry of the Book of Common Prayer. Baz, in days when he was still able to express his thoughts, had told me that when the day came he wanted a traditional funeral in St Peter's, just a few hundred steps from our front door, and I was happy with this. For me, church was all about the words and, especially, the music; not their religious connotations but the deep cultural well of beauty that they express. I wanted that now, and found the familiar rhythms soothing in my grief. Milly graciously stood by me as I made these choices, though I know that she herself has a visceral anger towards the church and its oppressive attitudes towards queer people. And from her point of view, not one of those cultural treasures could ever make up for that. Milly was deeply damaged by her experience of Christian teachings at school and in the cathedral, and I know now that the church is a very lonely place for people like her. It is yet another sign of her grace and strength that she was willing to stand beside me in making the funeral decisions, when every inch of her then and now quivers with violent antipathy to everything the church represents.

Day after day, florists' vans arrived at the house and the letter box heaved with cards. I was overwhelmed by the outpouring of friendship and support that flooded in. And when a beautiful handwritten letter from the Royal Society of Musicians arrived one day, I cried. They had, they wrote with great courtesy, heard from a colleague that caring for my husband through all these dreadful months had disastrously affected my ability to work and earn. Without any quibbling or bureaucracy, they enclosed a generous cheque and an offer of assistance for as long as I might need it in my time of crisis. The Royal Society of Musicians was founded in 1738 by Handel and other leading musicians of the day, and the contrast between their genuine, unstinting outreach and my distressing experiences of the social care system could not have been greater. I will always be grateful to them.

My mother had arrived from Australia and Leigh had flown over from Connecticut to join Milly. Lucas had crucial professional exams coming up and I did not want him to compromise them by flying back from Sydney. In any case, the last thing I needed right now was an undercurrent of conflict over the matter of Milly's transition. There was only so much I could cope with at one time, and I knew that Lucas, being Lucas, would maintain the rigour of his well-stated intellectual position no matter what the circumstances. It was, in truth, a relief not to have to deal with the added pressure any encounter between my two children would bring.

Other negotiations were required elsewhere too. Vicar wars had broken out in the village. I had asked my close friend Annie to conduct the service. Annie was a professional violinist whom I had worked with on and off for many years, and she had recently been ordained into the Church of England. Her patch was a neighbouring parish, and although the local vicar could hardly refuse my request, it wasn't long before he came calling, pushing more than I thought seemly for a role in the proceedings. I didn't know him and he didn't know me or, indeed, Baz, and so I held my ground stubbornly.

'I'm thinking that I could read the main part of the service and Annie could do the committal,' he said.

'No, I'm sorry, that doesn't work for me. Annie will take the service.'

'How about if I walk in behind the coffin reading the Sentences?'

'No, I'm sorry, that doesn't work for me.'

'I could give a reflection on his life and Annie could do a reading.' He was nothing if not persistent.

'No. I'm sorry, that doesn't work for me.'

Behind my sombre widow's demeanour, I found this tussling for sacred pole position darkly amusing, but in the interests of village harmony I eventually agreed that he could say one prayer.

I am not a churchgoer, but I am deeply cultural-ly embedded in the Church of England. Its music is one of the great glories of our civilisation and the Book of Common Prayer and the King James Bible are as monumental as the soaring gothic structures they echo around. Throughout the choir years, when I spent so many evenings in the college chapel, this rich tapestry of psalms and canticles, hymns and anthems had become part of the fabric of my life. For me, those musical splendours and honeyed words gave expression to nameless depths. This, I knew, would sustain me through the gruelling experience of bidding farewell to my husband's life and disposing of what was left of it. I set about organising the funeral and found attending to the details a welcome distraction as I measured every choice I made for its meaning and beauty. I wanted the occasion to have an elegant simplicity, raised aloft by music and readings, with white garden flowers decorating the ancient furnishings of the church and a single wreath on the coffin. But iron will and self-control can only get you so far, and on the morning of the funeral I woke heavy with a sense of dread. I felt sick to the stomach, nervous and agitated. I realised that the best way for me to survive this day with composure would be to treat it as a performance. I would lock the grief and trauma away for another, more private moment, and today I would hold myself high through my ordeal. I knew how to deal with performance nerves. Deep breath, head up, smile and out you go to face your audience.

The hearse arrived at the corner of the country lane outside our house. We gathered there, my mother, Milly, Leigh and I, along with the two Ollies, who had never failed in their support during Baz's final months. They were truly a part of this family of mourners. As we walked slowly behind the hearse along the tree-lined avenue that led up to the church, each of us was silent with our own thoughts. The morning was clear and bright, and the grass verges were awash with daffodils. The blackbirds sang in the hedgerow. Life was everywhere, rejoicing in itself and the irrepressible resurgence of spring. Not a car passed us as we walked along the long, gravelled path, nor another person as we drew near the lychgate where Annie stood waiting for us.

The others went forward into the cool darkness of the church, and for a moment my anxieties squirmed and shifted viscerally within me. Baz had been very much a part of village life, but my work and friendships largely lay elsewhere, and Milly, although now living at home again, hadn't really been seen out and about in the village since she had played with friends on the green as a young teenager. I suspected people might know about her transition, gossip being what it is, but if they did it wasn't because I had told them. My daughter paused to compose herself before walking into the church with all the self-assurance and dignity she could summon. I could tell that she was anxious about being out for the first time in this small, conservative community, dressed as a young woman in mourning. She didn't want to draw any attention to herself, especially when it was Baz who was at the heart of this day, but she had made an inviolable pact with herself, an unmovable commitment to her transition, and so she bravely squared herself to her fear of stares and mockery in the midst of her grief. She would not let pointing fingers undermine the meaning of what we were all going through. Leigh, at Milly's side, was dressed in her own uniquely individual interpretation of suitable funeral style, accessorised with Doc Marten boots and purple hair, and she took Milly's arm to support her as they walked in together. Edwards and Dawson followed behind, their heavy metal credentials loosely concealed by sober suits. I was proud of them all, this motley crew around me, though I felt sure that Little Heywick had never before seen a procession like it.

And then it was time. The pallbearers lifted the coffin and I closed my eyes, trying not to imagine the jutting bones and ashen flesh that lay within as I walked slowly behind. The memory of that desperate, breathing skeleton was all too close in my nightmares. Annie briefly squeezed my hand and I was grateful for her gentle gesture of friendship. When we entered the church, my heart was overwhelmed. It was full, and in the candlelit transept colleagues and students had gathered to play together. The music of Fauré breathed and swelled, echoing in the stones, and I knew that each one of these friends was there for me. As so often on this long journey of death and rebirth, I was humbled by love.

'Man that is born of a woman hath but a short time to live,' Annie intoned as we processed down the aisle. 'He cometh up and is cut down like a flower and never continueth in one stay.'

How true, how beautiful, how sad. It was all too short; life, in every moment, was its own greatest gift to us. To live life to the full was not to be faint-hearted.

'Like as the hart desireth the waterbrooks, so longeth my soul after thee, O God.' The words of the psalm resonated in their mysterious beauty. 'One deep calleth another, because of the noise of thy waterfloods; all thy waves and storms are gone over me.'

We sang, and favourite hymns and the sound of the organ rang in the rafters; prayers were said and the eulogy given. And then it was my turn. I would not, I had decided, speak of Baz or reflect on his life. Instead, I would read from the Song of Songs. Many years before, I had written my thesis on this mystical masterpiece, a journey through text and symbol that had changed the direction of my own life by bringing me to Cambridge. I loved the cadence of the phrases, the enigmatic language and its evocation of the bonds that connect us. Especially now, it spoke to me, of love and loss, of the tide of life and of new beginnings. For me, there were no other words more right for this springtime passing.

'Rise up and come away,' I read, and my voice momentarily faltered. I looked out over the collected faces before me, the friends and strangers, the wreaths of country flowers, the simple oak coffin. I breathed to steady myself; I could do this.

'For, lo, the winter is past, the rain is over and gone; the flowers appear on the earth.'

And I knew that they would, that the cycle would continue. Change is our biggest fear and yet, so often, when we have the courage to accept it with grace, it is also the opportunity of our greatest freedom. There are always new beginnings. Baz had gone, too soon but at least in the natural order of things; and Amelie had been born, too late and against that natural order. But our capacity to embrace whatever change comes to us is what makes us grow. In this way we ourselves take charge of our direction in life, setting our sail against the slower death of stagnation in a safe harbour.

In the bright sunlight outside the church, I stood again at the lychgate and greeted all the friends and colleagues, villagers and relatives as they came through it. It struck me, as I stood there shaking hands, receiving embraces and condolences, that it was rather like some monstrously inverted wedding.

'Thank you so much for coming.'

'Wonderful service... lovely flowers...'

'Thank you so much for coming.'

'Dinner soon...'

'Thank you. Thank you so much for coming.'

Small clusters of mourners stood around in the churchyard, catching up on other news, and Milly, Leigh and the Ollies waited by the hearse where the coffin rested again. Nearby, someone from the village, someone who had probably last seen Milly in the days when she was Miles, lazily kicking a ball on the village green, glanced in her direction and said to no one in particular, 'Good God, what a show. Glad Baz never lived to see the day...' Quick as a whip, Edwards turned around. 'He'd turn in his grave, would he? Oh, wait...'

'Bravo,' I muttered under my breath. 'Well played.' Milly kept her head high, eyes fixed on the coffin, and did not flinch.

The rest of the day passed as these occasions always

do. The coffin was taken to the crematorium. In the village hall, pots of tea and plates of cake were laid out by friends. Wine was shared, past times recollected. Milly stayed only five minutes at the hall; the incident outside the church had spoilt her appetite for sandwiches and small talk. I was exhausted to my bones by the effort of it all and wished I could go home too.

It was late afternoon by the time the last friends and relatives had drifted away and the hall had been tidied up. At home, I sat in the kitchen with my mother, Milly and Leigh, surrounded by remnants of sandwiches and cakes, too tired to do more than just rest my head in my hands. 'Baz would have been proud of you today,' my mother said. 'It was a beautiful service. Everything was perfect.'

'I'm glad it's over.'

'Definitely the best funeral I've ever been to,' she mused. 'It was just like being in an episode of *Downton Abbey*.'

And then after a while, as darkness fell, only Milly and I were left. Milly's face was etched with the strain of the day and she seemed to be grappling with something just out of reach as she fidgeted and noodled on her guitar. We sat, keeping each other company and not saying much; a glass of wine for me, a peppermint tea for Milly. I could sense that the depression she had managed to hold at bay for some time now was once again not far away. It was understandable, of course, after the events of the day, but I wasn't sure that her heaviness came only from the stress and grief. She seemed too lost in her own thoughts. 'Baz didn't do a lot of the things he wanted to do,' she said. It was true. Baz was always preparing for tomorrow rather than living for today; and then he died, and all those future plans were unfulfilled. Tomorrow would never come for him.

I flicked listlessly through the pile of mail that had built up over the past few days. More cards, more handwritten envelopes; how kind. Bills, solicitors' letters, bank statements, notifications, forms. There is so much to do when someone dies. 'One for you,' I said, tossing an envelope towards Milly. I knew she would not be happy to see it addressed to Mr Miles Martin. She tore it open angrily, taking in its contents in a glance, and I could see that a wave of fury had come over her. She heaved with sobs as she threw it down on the table, and all the despair of absolutely everything flooded out. 'What is it?' I asked anxiously. 'What's happened?'

'It's from the Tavistock and Portman,' she said, gulping with sobs. 'The Gender Identity Clinic in London. They've finally sent me my first appointment date. For a psychiatric assessment.'

'Well, that's good news, isn't it? I mean, I'm very surprised that the GIC of all places hasn't got your name right. But at least you've finally got your appointment.'

'Oh yes, brilliant. It's next year. Eighteen months from now.'

It was already more than a year since Milly had come out. A year of constant hoop-jumping as she met one criterion after another. Out to family, out to friends, out to work, her name changed by deed poll, living and presenting in her new gender role, counselling sessions, psychotherapists' letters. Tick, tick, tick. Already four months since her doctor had first referred her to the Charing Cross GIC for an initial consultation. And today she had been insulted by a stranger at the funeral of the man she called her father. Milly couldn't wait another year and a half; she couldn't wait another day. Milly's transition issues had taken a backseat for a while now as I grappled with Baz's illness and death and its aftermath, but now, with impeccably inappropriate timing, they needed to be faced again.

'I'm way past this,' she said, trembling between fury and despair. 'I've jumped through every one of their hoops to be eligible for the hormones, and this is what I get. Back to the end of the queue, step in line for stage one. I'm done. I don't need the GIC. There are other ways to get them. Illegal hormones. Internet pharmacies. Self-medication.'

I was horrified. 'Milly, no. You're talking about taking risks with your life. We will find a way through this, I promise, but please, not tonight.' The funeral had taken the very last vestiges of my emotional and physical reserves. All I could think about was escaping into sleep, to rest and gather myself for the first day of my new life.

I had thought that the task of beginning again would start with getting some semblance of normality and balance back into my daily routine. Now, apparently, it would also include finding a way through the labyrinthine world of medical gender transition, knocking on doors until we could find someone who would answer my daughter's cry for help.

CHAPTER 13

Amelie, I soon discovered, was far from alone in her desperation. The waiting time for a first appointment with the Charing Cross Gender Identity Clinic in London was then around eighteen months from initial referral (now it is three years), and even longer at the other clinics around the country. Nationally, referrals outstrip available appointments by four to one, and a shortage of clinical specialists in the field of gender identity means that there are thousands of people on waiting lists at each of these centres. In Leeds, in the north of England, patients are advised to expect a five-year wait for hormones; in the south-west, the Devon clinic has a four-and-a-half-year wait just for an initial screening appointment. Across Europe and most of the English-speaking world, the story is much the same: woeful ignorance of gender dysphoria and transgender healthcare issues is widespread among family medical practitioners, and there is currently no medical training route that prepares doctors for specialisation in gender affirmation medicine and surgery. Consequently, the wait for diagnosis and hormones is long and the prospect of finally undergoing sex reassignment surgery vanishingly distant. The picture so often painted in the media of young people being given hormones and referred for life-changing surgery at the merest flicker of interest in pink trainers and Barbie dolls (or their boyish equivalents) is a scaremongering fallacy that says far more about the people propagating this myth than it does about the teenagers and families who are so anxiously seeking help.

In any case, referral for a first appointment does not, as Milly had thought when she tore open that letter, offer any immediate hope of hormone therapy. After an initial screening interview, there is another wait of at least a year for assessment and medical diagnosis. To receive hormones from an endocrinologist, a formal diagnosis of gender identity disorder must first be made, requiring yet more counselling and further letters of confirmation. The prescription for the drugs which will finally begin the longed-for medical transition is only given at the third appointment, another year or more down the line. The process is torturously slow, and in a community already disproportionately affected by depression, self-harm and suicide, the wait for treatment, and the lack of any support or communication in the meantime, can be devastating and even dangerous. In an attempt to work around some of these problems, a hopelessly paradoxical catch-22 has been created whereby GPs are allowed to prescribe 'bridging hormones' if they believe a patient with gender dysphoria is seriously at risk of suicide or is self-medicating with hormones bought online. Good news. Except, most GPs do not feel (probably correctly) that they have the experience to prescribe such hormone treatment – and providing ongoing monitoring of the hormone levels in the blood also worries many doctors, who are concerned about managing abnormal results and the possibility of litigation if anything goes wrong under their care. So, what do they do? They approach the gender specialists for advice and at the same time refer their patient onto the Gender Identity Clinic pathway. And as soon as a patient is on the waiting list for the GIC, they are no longer eligible for bridging hormones. No wonder web-based pharmacies in places like India and Vanuatu have a thriving business in exporting private sources of oestrogen, anti-androgens and testosterone.

Milly was quite beside herself at the dawning realisation that all her efforts over the past year counted for little in terms of getting to her end goal of full medical and surgical transition. She was stuck in a holding pattern, one of the many thousands falling so far outside the treatment capacity of the NHS gender clinics that, for them, progress seems hopeless. I watched her mental state plunge precipitously over the next few days as we spent hours researching alternatives together, and I worried wretchedly for her. Milly was adamant that self-medication was the only way out of her dilemma. Around a third of all trans women are already taking hormones purchased online by the time they are first seen at a clinic, but what I read about the subject worried me deeply. There is a wealth of information available on the internet for those who are driven to these measures: easy-to-find websites provide comprehensive prescription protocols, as well as links to amenable suppliers. The cost is not unfeasible, and with a few clicks you can be on your way, leapfrogging that impossible queue with your future back in your own hands. I could see why it was tempting. But hormone therapy requires close monitoring through regular blood tests, and over- and under-dosing both have their risks, all of which are helpfully spelled out on the websites, of course, along with some strong disclaimers. Most worrying to me were the repeated warnings that the testosterone-blocker cyproterone acetate can cause severe depression. Knowing Milly's history of depression, the possibility of making it worse did not seem like a good idea to me at all. Milly, though, was prepared to risk this side effect regardless of her susceptibility, and she brushed away the warnings. It also worried me that the drugs, turning up in unmarked packages from the other side of the world, might not even be what they claimed to be. I knew there was a trade in counterfeit drugs (of all kinds) from China, and so that possibility seemed quite likely. Desperate people do desperate things, but this was my daughter and I would do anything I could to stop her being driven to this dangerous last resort.

A week after Baz's funeral we were back at the kitchen table, weighing up the options. 'There *are* no options,' Milly said. She had sunk into a very low mood again, and I mobilised every spark of enthusiasm I could muster to give her something to hold on to. 'There is another way,' I replied. 'You could see an endocrinologist privately. Get started on the hormones outside the system but still under the care of a specialist. That way, you'd be making progress while you wait for the next stage appointment with the GIC. And when you finally get to that appointment, you can slip back into the system.' I didn't know if that part was true, but it was worth a try.

'How can I afford it?' Milly asked hopelessly. 'You know I don't have private health cover, and even if I did, the chances of them covering trans healthcare are next to zero.'

This was true, and right now I didn't have an answer. 'We can worry about that later. The first step is to go back to Dr Thompson and get a referral to a private specialist. In fact, you should do the research. She might not be so up to speed on this. You need to find out who's the best – who you want to see – and then ask the

doctor for a referral to that person. Take back control.'
A new light of tentative optimism seemed to flicker in
Milly's eyes.

'I've already had appointments at the surgery and
got nowhere. Dr Phillips tried to refer me to a mental
health unit, and Dr Samuels thought I needed therapy
to talk about being gay.' I did know that she had got off
on the wrong foot at the local surgery, but lately Milly
had found a new ally in Dr Thompson, who had been
very helpful. It was Dr Thompson who, with the best
of intentions, had finally referred her to the Charing
Cross clinic, which at the time had seemed a major step
forward.

'If you want me to come with you to fight your corner,
make an appointment and we'll go together.' My sense
of being totally at sea in this new world had not abated,
so I hardly thought I could bring any authority to the
occasion, but if Milly needed support to articulate her
concerns and get the help she needed, then I would be
there with her. Perhaps my presence could simply give
her strength and the confidence that she was being
taken seriously. And, if nothing else, recent experience
meant she knew that I really was very good at standing
up to doctors whom I didn't see eye to eye with.

Before the appointment, I tried to learn as much as
I could about the hormone treatment Milly needed so
that I wasn't left floundering in the discussion. There
are two essential elements in male-to-female hormone

therapy: firstly, Milly would need to take an anti-androgen like cyproterone acetate to block the production of testosterone, and secondly, alongside that, an oestrogen to feminise her hormone profile. She would need monthly blood tests at first, and then every three months, to monitor her testosterone and oestrogen, and to check her liver function and iron and B12 levels, which can all be affected by the anti-androgens. She would have to keep an eye on her blood pressure, and blood clots would be a significant risk. Hormone dosage would need to be carefully controlled around any kind of surgery and before long-haul flights. In short, I was very glad I'd managed to convince her that she should at least try to have a specialist oversee her hormone therapy, instead of self-medicating. This was not something to be taken lightly.

Dr Thompson was welcoming but serious as Milly explained why she had made the appointment and why she had asked me to come with her. I was quick to stress that I understood that Milly was responsible for her own healthcare decisions and that I was there simply to support her by confirming how desperate I knew this situation had become. Milly was almost at breaking point with despair, I told the doctor. I was worried for her mental health and for her safety. Milly kept her eyes down, allowing her long hair to fall forward and hide her face. She still found interacting with people a source of great anxiety, especially when her gender dysphoria was heightened, as it was at the moment. 'Milly, can you tell me in your own words how you are feeling?' Dr Thompson asked gently.

It all came out in a rush. 'I'm at the end of the road. I've been waiting and waiting and hoping and hoping, and now I find out it's going to be years... literally years... before I have a chance of starting on hormones. I've always felt this way. I've been unhappy my whole life. Everything about me is wrong. The way I look, the way I sound, the shape of my body. I look at myself naked and I feel completely revolted. I want nothing to do with this flesh, this shape, these... these append-ages. I want them gone. They disgust me. I disgust myself. The only way I can survive is if I can change my body, and if I can't get hormones legally, I will get them online. It's either that or I have no future to look forward to. I really think it's the only choice I have left.' Once the tap of her despair had been turned on there was no stopping it, and her words and distress came flooding out. I thought I had known her pain, but this anguish plumbed a new depth. I was shocked by her passion and the extremity of her misery.

'Thank you, Milly,' Dr Thompson said quietly, as her words finally petered out into exhausted sobs. 'You've been very eloquent, and I'm sorry you haven't yet had the care you need and deserve. I will refer you to a private endocrinologist. You will have to pay for the consultation, but at least it will get things underway. Once the consultant assesses you and decides on the proper hormone regime for you, we can take over prescribing them here at the surgery.'

Milly was shaking with emotion. 'Thank you, thank you, thank you,' she kept repeating. 'Thank you so much.'

'I'll do some research on the best person to refer you to,' Dr Thompson continued, 'and will call you tomorrow so that you can make the appointment as soon as possible.'

Dr Thompson was as good as her word, and by the next afternoon Milly was beaming. She now had a consultation with Professor James Frost, an eminent endocrinologist at a private hospital in Cambridge, pencilled in her diary just a month away. The cost would run into hundreds of pounds, but set against what she would have spent on privately acquired hormones the equation balanced without causing her too much financial concern. At last I could see the dawn of real hope in her eyes.

As the days went by, Milly had a constant fizz of excitement about her, but there was still an undercurrent of nervousness in her demeanour. Her hopes were high but grounded in realism, and she expected the first meeting with Professor Frost to be a formality; the prescription, she thought, would still be months away. Milly's experiences had left her extremely mistrustful of the healthcare system in general, and as a trans woman, she felt her medical needs were secondary or even invisible.

I noticed something very strange about Milly's musicianship during this period of limbo. Her creative life drew to a complete halt. I could hear the stagnation in her playing, and there was a striking disconnect between her technical ability and her expression. In essence, she stopped playing music. She did not stop *playing* – that would be inconceivable – and if anything, she became even more fanatical in her hours of practice, but during that period of waiting I never heard a single melody emerge from the studio. Milly completely stopped learning new styles and songs, gave up composing and improvising and put aside jamming for the sheer pleasure of it. Instead, she regimented herself with ten unremitting hours of technique practice every day. It sounded joyless in its repetitive rigidity; I never heard the intense discipline relieved even for a moment by music taking flight in the unbridled exhilaration of playing. To me this change said something about what was going on inside her and it worried me greatly. I couldn't understand why she had closed down like this musically when music had always been her one trusted place. After a week of listening to her new routine thrum constantly in the background, I decided I had to say something to her. 'Milly,' I began, carefully weighing my words (no musician likes to be told how to practise), 'do you think it's a good idea to spend so many hours on exercises every day? I mean, yes, it's great to work on your technique, but this is relentless. You could damage yourself if you carry on like this. And you're never actually playing any music. There's no point in doing technique exercises just for the sake of it; they're to make you a better musician not a better technician.'

'It's the only way I can cope right now.' she replied. 'My anxiety is so bad that it's completely blocked my connection with the music. I feel like I've lost the ability to express myself. This is all I can do.' Ah, stupid me, of course. It was just like when she used to line up those train engines as a child or work out in the gym as a teenager; a rigid obsession with orderliness and categories and schedules was how Milly coped when life was spinning out of control. By playing endless scales, modes, arpeggios and chords in all their myriad configurations, commanding them with a metronome, and shaping them with different picking styles, Milly kept the world at bay; she was comforted and soothed by the repetition. 'I hope I can find it again,' she said, 'but I just don't know. I don't know what the hormones will do to me emotionally. But physically and mentally, I've got no choice. I can't wait to start them – but I'm scared too.' So was I.

When the day of the appointment finally arrived three weeks later, Milly was a bundle of nervous energy. She paced up and down the music studio, practising her vocal exercises and pausing occasionally to release her fevered excitement and anxiety on her guitar. This time I was not going to go with Milly to her consultation. She was adamant that she wanted to face this momentous hurdle alone, and so I was left to do my own pacing and practising. I was distracted as my imagination veered wildly from the ramifications for Milly if the longed-for drugs were refused through to the bewildering unknown of her future if they were prescribed. Not for the first time, I felt a hopeless failure as a mother. I knew that this was my child's greatest desire and her most desperate need, and yet I found it terrifying to contemplate.

'You'll be fine,' I said. 'Just go in there and tell him everything.'

The appointment seemed to go on a long time. And then there she was in the doorway, glowing with a halo of joy. 'I've got them,' she said, her voice quivering with disbelief. 'I've got them. The hormone prescription. He's given it to me today. Today! I can actually go to the pharmacy and get them.'

Milly was exuberant and nothing could quench the unstoppable flow of her delight. She was bursting at the seams. 'My heart won't stop pounding. I just couldn't believe my ears when he said it,' she exclaimed breathlessly. The words tumbled out with excitement. 'When I got there it was so strange; I was definitely the only trans person there. I felt really out of place.' Apparently, the hormonal causes of obesity, rather than transgenderism, was one of Professor Frost's famed areas of expertise. Milly would have looked a fish out of water among them with her youthful looks, slim build and pretty dress.

'He said to me, "You are by no means the first person who's come to me to about this and you certainly won't be the first or the last that I've prescribed these medications to." And then he wrote me the prescription. I don't even have to see him again for three months.'

Still spinning with excitement, Milly headed straight to the nearest pharmacy, but was crushed to find them out of stock. 'Not something we normally carry, umm… madam,' said the assistant, glancing quizzically at the prescription then at Milly. Her medical records still carried her former name, yet another obstacle to be navigated as she skirted around the endless gatekeepers she encountered at every step of her journey. But this time Milly was prepared to wait. I was surprised by her patience and even more by the clarity and calm of her thought process: she might be in orbit with elation but she had enough composure to know that if one pharmacy didn't have it, this not being an everyday request, it was likely she would also have to wait at any other pharmacy. She placed her order and was assured that she would receive the drugs in five days' time, and that was good enough for Milly. After a lifetime of waiting, what were a few more days? At last, she would have the hormones that would help her change her body and her life, and in this way she saw for the first time the real and tangible possibility of achieving happiness and comfort. One day, one day soon, she would be passable. One day, she might be happy.

CHAPTER 14

No matter what happened in Milly's life, for her there was only one way to celebrate, retreat, heal or mourn. The guitar was her voice and the prism through which she expressed her inner self; this was why I had been so worried by the rigidity I had heard in her music lately. I was well attuned to what Milly was saying or not saying when she played. As soon as she got back from town, blown joyfully homeward on the day's endocrinology whirlwind, Milly hit the music studio with her favourite guitar, the black seven-string Ibanez she called Alice. Out poured one favourite solo after another, speaking of emotions suspended somewhere between sadness and rage, of potential that could only be unlocked by the intense virtuosity of these fiery outpourings. Today, for Milly, the music was back.

In other respects, though, her celebration was, for a 22-year-old, a very sober affair. Having put aside her

bodybuilding and meat-filled diet and adopted veganism in the pursuit of a feminised body, Milly lives an
ascetic life in other ways. She doesn't touch alcohol,
smoke or use recreational drugs; even coffee is off
limits. An intensive session on the frets and a cup of
peppermint tea marked the zenith of Milly's excitement
and, for her, that was more than enough. Milly's life-
style was curiously at odds with the usual stereotypes
expected of rock or jazz musicians, or even with those
of the average session musician, and she was religious
in adhering to her monastic habits. Alcohol, smoking
and coffee would all, she had been told, affect to a
greater or lesser degree the uptake of the hormones or
increase the risk of their possible dangerous side effects,
and so she abstained. Fortunately, she had no interest
in them anyway and so they were easily struck off her
list of vices. The vegan diet, she believed, would give her
the best baseline health-wise to pursue her transition
and so, again, that was not negotiable. But she also
embraced veganism from an ethical standpoint: having
experienced so much suffering in her own life, she was
adamant that she could not in turn cause suffering
to other creatures. Even spiders had to be allowed to
live unmolested in their webs if they set up home in
the corner of her bedroom during the summer months.
Everything Milly did in life was in some way related to
her quest to escape from the grotesque insult her body
had imposed upon her, whether it was by ensuring she

was in optimum health or by her empathy for the pain of others or by giving voice to her creative flow.

The five-day wait for the hormones passed in a tide of music and happiness. In between gigs and teaching, Milly played and practised and chatted cheerfully to me about guitars and hormones, her two favourite subjects. I now knew more about what she had been prescribed. Professor Frost had given Milly the anti-androgen cyproterone acetate as a testosterone-blocker, prescribing her a dose that was double the usual amount. In Europe, cyproterone acetate is the standard T-blocker, but in the US and many other countries it is a controlled substance, and so spironolactone is used instead. Both drugs are toxic long term and both have serious side effects: cypro causes depression and spiro causes potassium build-up and other problems. Milly didn't care; the high-dose anti-androgen would start acting immediately, finally calling a halt to the masculinising effect of testosterone in her system.

When it came to the feminising hormones, Professor Frost's prescription of a combination of ethinyl estradiol and progesterone was a bit old-school. Ethinyl estradiol is a synthetic hormone that is more potent than naturally occurring oestrogen and carries a significantly higher risk of blood clotting. Most physicians now prescribe the more recently developed bioidentical oestrogens, such as estradiol valerate, and a couple of years down the line that is what Milly takes. She will be on this medication for the rest of her life. Along with the oestrogen, Milly was offered progesterone, although Professor Frost's view was that there was little evidence that this would add anything to the effectiveness of the regime. Some think, he told her, that it helps with breast development. 'I'll take it,' said Milly.

The moment when Milly finally went to collect her prescription was a surprisingly solemn one for both of us. She seemed quite overwhelmed at the immensity of what was about to happen and was taciturn as she went out the door. 'See you soon,' I called after her. 'Good luck.'

'Hmm,' she said. With her eyes down and her hair over her face, Milly was hiding herself even from me, and I briefly wondered what change I might see on the other side of her short journey to the chemist. Short in miles, but so very long in coming. I could understand why she was stunned into silence by the momentous nature of this simple errand. I felt a shift in the world as I knew it too. Now, Milly's body would begin to alter; she would become infertile and I would never see the grandchildren that might have been. Until this moment, although I had never for a moment considered that she might change her mind, or even (once I got used to the idea) wished for it, the steps that Milly had taken towards becoming a woman had been superficial and reversible. She could go back to wearing men's clothes, lower the pitch of her voice, reclaim her old name. But today she was taking the first step towards irrevocably changing her physiology, and from this point there really was no turning back. I was happy for my daughter's happiness but anxious for her health. I was also unsettled by the knowledge that together we were headed into the unknown, into a future that, for me if not for Milly, looked backward into loss as well as forward into the promise of a new beginning.

During the first months of her medical transition, the stage of the transition process where hormone therapy begins, Milly kept a video diary to record the changes that she felt and saw in herself. I knew of it but never watched it, of course, and that seemed right to me. For Milly, this video diary was a very private combination of reflection and personal documentary, and through it she hoped to be able to remind herself how far she had come every time either gender dysphoria or depression threatened to destabilise her confidence and sense of progress. My personal encounter with Milly's transition on hormones could only be that of an observer, but to me it seemed that she became noticeably more gentle, more empathetic, more interested in nuance. She was, I thought, more attuned to life's undercurrents of heartache and joy. I was also very curious to know what changes Milly noticed in herself, and during that period of change I often talked to her about what she was experiencing physically and emotionally. Certainly the constant depression had lifted and she seemed to have a new aura of hope around her, but I could see that there was much more going on.

Milly told me that all her sensations became heightened once she was taking the hormones. 'I've just become more sensitive to everything,' she said. 'I can feel the wind on my face and the clothes on my skin. I'm aware of colours, and everything seems brighter. I'm noticing textures and tasting food in ways that I never did before. For the first time, I can really understand the pleasure in eating.' She became more experimental with food and clothes, starting to wear colour and pattern instead of her usual black, and enjoying new flavours and styles of cooking. 'Until now, it was as if life was in black and white,' she told me. 'Everything was dulled. But now I feel like the world is alive and I am happy to be alive in it.' Milly also became noticeably more emotional and she told me that in private she often cried out of sheer happiness. Cuteness now appealed to her in a way that it never had before, and the sight of an adorable kitten or an endearing toddler could bring tears to her eyes. And she would cry at films. *Guardians of the Galaxy II* left her weeping hopelessly in the cinema, as the protagonist's psychodrama with his father reminded her of the absence and failings of her own father and of the loss of Baz. All Milly's emotions were more raw and nearer the surface than she had ever allowed before. I ask myself whether this was because it was her way of exploring for the first time what she perceived to be womanly emotions or if it was merely because her body was in hormonal turmoil, or if it was something more fundamental. I have no way of knowing the answer, but I cannot deny the emotional experience, whatever its basis.

One of the first things I did when Milly started changing hormonally and looking ever more feminine was talk to her about the dangers of being a woman. My daughter had been a tall, muscular youth who could walk the streets with all the subconscious confidence that comes from knowing you are unlikely to be the first choice of a passing thug and in the knowledge that if you were, you stood an even chance of coming off the better. Hours every day in the gym had given that young male body an obvious physical advantage which simply added to the intrinsic advantage of masculinity. Men don't have to learn how to stay safe from predators when they take their first independent steps into the world. But girls do, and I was worried that Milly had missed out on that vital socialisation. I soon realised that Milly was way ahead of me on this (as usual, I suppose). She was acutely aware of her vulnerability and the dangers she faced as a trans woman. The risk of abuse and assault was constantly with her and, if anything, I discovered it had given her a great empathy for the risks women face from potential aggressions, large and small. Somewhere in us all, we keep an awareness of the danger tucked away as we go about our daily lives, and that resonated with Milly.

One of the most frequently voiced concerns of people who hold strong views about trans women and their claim to womanhood is that places where women typically feel 'exposed', like public toilets and changing rooms, should be off limits to those they consider to be fraudulent intruders into their space. Some are willing to make an exception for post-operative trans women, but as there is no courteous way to ask to check someone's genitals, this is a bit problematic. I have come to think of this anxiety as the Little Red Riding Hood fallacy. It is the primal terror of discovering that Grandma is really the Big Bad Wolf. Women who fear the ingress of trans women into female-only 'safe spaces' are not afraid of trans women; they are afraid of men. And many of them may rightly be so. The domestic violence sufferer or the rape survivor does not necessarily carry the badge of her abuse, but she is deeply scarred by it. But what I have learnt from seeing my daughter transition is that, leaving aside the long inner suffering that would surely affect the essence of anyone's being, leaving aside arguments about the innateness or otherwise of gender, once you start taking those testosterone-blockers the speed at which the body physically weakens is remarkable. Muscles atrophy and the genitals wither and the power of masculinity soon becomes mostly impotent. A trans woman on hormones does not have the physical capacity to be a danger in the way her formerly testosterone-ridden body might have allowed, and in any case, there is also good scientific evidence that androgen-blockers inhibit aggressive behaviour.

Of course, I realise that just as the status of the genitals is not immediately obvious (and why should it be?), neither can you know if someone is medically transitioning with hormone treatment or not. Equally, I can only speculate that the number of real aggressors who might use a feminine disguise to gain access to vulnerable women is very small compared to the number of genuine transgender women, at whatever stage of transition, who only seek to be themselves, living in peace and being accepted with courtesy. It seems to me that there is no need for a man to cunningly 'self-ID', as it is now known, to be a danger to a woman. They can do it anywhere and, if so inclined, they do. The wolf can lurk and pounce from behind a tree as swiftly and easily as he can when disguised as Grandma in her bedroom. In fact, the danger to a trans woman of being forced to use male facilities is, I believe, far greater than the danger to women of a trans woman using female facilities. It is also a legal conundrum: the internationally accepted rules on medical and surgical transition require a transitioning individual to live and work in their affirmed gender full-time for at least a year before they can be considered for treatment. If a trans woman must present as a woman in all aspects of daily life, how can it be acceptable that she should be forced either by law or by society to use the male toilets?

My view of this vexed issue is coloured by the upsetting memory of Milly's experience at a Berlin television station, where she was performing on a popular German music programme not long after she came out. Backstage, she was offered use of either the men's or women's changing rooms but was told plainly by some of the women that she was not welcome in their space. The men, overhearing this, said she could use their changing room, but the confrontation had made her panicky and breathless with anxiety. Milly decided that she would get changed in the disabled toilet instead, but even there she was not safe. While she was in the cubicle, a group of women (astonishingly, from the team she was working with) repeatedly tried to kick the door in. She was terrified and stayed locked in the toilet until they finally left her alone. After that, Milly kept to herself on the tour. If this can happen to someone who is a performer working on an international television show, surrounded by managers and minders, how much more likely is this kind of toilet terrorism for someone simply going about their everyday life at the local gym or shopping centre?

As for my own observations when Milly started taking the hormones, it didn't take me long to recognise startling changes in her. As the weeks went by, something about her whole demeanour became less defined, her edges more yielding, as if seen through gauze. Her skin glowed and her hair shone. Her breasts began to develop, even if only a little at first. Her masculine musculature melted away, and in general there was a softening of the body and a tenderness to its shape that had not previously been there. Most striking to me, though, was the very real change in the relationship between us. Milly, as Miles, had always been withdrawn and downcast, but our relationship was nonetheless affectionate and, or so I had thought, approachable. But what I found now was that, to my great surprise, I started to relate to this new incarnation of Milly in a strikingly changed way. There was a new dynamic between us as mother and daughter, and this relationship came with ease. I am not talking about an experience based on girly explorations of femininity; it was a depth of mutual understanding. We could now talk in a way that was palpably different to that which I had experienced as the mother of sons. I was both fascinated and troubled by this change, not wishing to essentialise gender or to subscribe to biologically deterministic arguments about the nature of the 'female brain'. That position seemed to me to be worryingly anti-feminist, and yet here I was experiencing my child as a medically induced daughter and, I have to say, it was fundamentally different. Was it simply because Milly could now allow herself to express what she perceived to be appropriate gender stereotypes in terms of how she related to me? Possibly, and

I know some will argue that case, but I don't think so. The change was so palpable, deep and vivid that I was very affected by it. It was at this point in Milly's transition that I found myself able to say for the first time 'I have a daughter' and to know, in my heart, that this was the truth.

CHAPTER 15

As Milly settled into the hormone regime, her joy in all the changes it brought did not ultimately give her ease. Rather, it simply meant that the focus of her body dysmorphia shifted to other tell-tale signs of her natal sex. So far, she had changed the way she dressed, her name, her voice, her male musculature. She had permanently removed her facial and body hair. The hormones had softened her skin and given her the beginning of curves. But the more closely her emotions and new femininity corresponded to her own body image, the starker the remaining masculine character-istics became in her eyes. Milly detested her Adam's apple (which, in fact, was not particularly pronounced) and these days she always covered it with a scarf. Now, having succeeded in her quest for hormone therapy, she turned her indefatigable pursuit of womanliness to this abhorrent piece of cartilage.

'There's an operation I can have to remove it,' she told me one day when she was having one of her I'm-not-passing moments. 'I want to have it done.' The very thought of it made my hand spring involuntarily to my throat. 'I've been researching it and there are surgeons that specialise in facial feminisation.'

'On the NHS?' I asked.

'No. The NHS won't cover it. It's plastic surgery. But it's not about vanity,' she added quickly. 'It's about alleviating the dysphoria. And for me, it's about passing. It's about getting rid of the constant anxiety, the fear of leaving the house without covering my neck. Every time I look at myself, the sight of my throat horrifies me. Actually, I can barely look at myself at all. When I see it, it's just one more reminder of all the wrongness. I've got to fix it, otherwise I'll never be comfortable with how I look.'

This was the first time I had heard of this aspect of transition and, quite apart from the cost implications of more private treatment, I had many concerns. I hate the thought of surgery at any time and found it even harder to contemplate for something that to me seemed merely cosmetic. To me, through the eyes of a mother, Milly already looked perfect, but I knew that she was driven by deep-seated needs that were beyond my understanding. I also knew that on the hormones Milly was at particular risk of blood clots and that controlling that risk would mean endocrinology work before any surgery. It all struck me as painful, desperate and expensive, but Milly was immoveable.

'I've found out that if I have it done abroad it will be cheaper,' she said. 'I've found a clinic in Spain and one in Poland. And there's one in Belgium. I'm going to email them all and get quotes.'

It sounded terribly commercial, and the horrifying experience at the laser hair removal clinic had made me very aware that glossy publicity is no assurance of quality of care. Milly showed me stylish websites with before and after images of beautiful women, trans women with Adam's apples and then without, women with other types of facial reconstruction. I closed my eyes to those ones. I really was frightened that Milly was about to head down a rabbit hole of perpetual plastic surgery, striving for some mythical ideal of feminine beauty. She assured me that this was not the case, but on the matter of the thyroid cartilage reduction surgery, also known as chondrolaryngoplasty or the tracheal shave, she was adamant. The Adam's apple is a secondary sexual characteristic in men that develops in adolescence in response to the testosterone that floods the body at puberty. It protects the front of the larynx, including the vocal cords; women also have one, although in females it remains unobtrusive because their different hormonal profile does not spike its growth. In males, the thickening of the thyroid cartilage prominence creates a soundboard that gives men their deeper vocal pitch, although once puberty has taken place, thinning the cartilage will not raise it. Chondrolaryngoplasty, so Milly told me, is a fairly simple procedure in which the surgeon shaves away the cartilage through a keyhole incision made under the chin, until it is as thin as possible. It still sounded appalling to me, but I'm squeamish.

In the end, we found ourselves back in Harley Street. Milly had done her research thoroughly and had decided that the clinic she wanted to use was in Brussels. Belgium was more expensive than Spain or Poland (although still much cheaper than England), but Milly thought, and I was quick to agree, that it was better to choose the surgeon with the best references and most experience. Dr van den Berg held a London clinic in Harley Street once a month to consult with British patients desperate for a place on the waiting list for surgery in his Brussels clinic, and once again I went to the appointment with Milly. It was a Sunday morning and London was quiet as we headed to the gracious Georgian building that was home to Dr van den Berg's temporary rooms. The comfortable waiting room was strewn with albums full of photos of the surgeon's success stories, and Milly flicked through them anxiously. Other women with Adam's apples or heavy features soon arrived, and there was an air of general agitation coupled with anticipation.

'Amelie?' An elegantly dressed man appeared at a door off the waiting room, and Milly got up.

'Come with me, please,' she whispered. 'I'm nervous. I need you.'

I was nervous too. It all seemed so very strange to me, finding myself in the heart of this world, a world I hadn't even known existed. But Dr van den Berg was charming and Milly quickly relaxed as she described the feelings of revulsion her Adam's apple induced and her desperation to have it removed. I think the doctor could see how anxious I was, sitting there in the corner of the consulting room, and he turned to me. 'I see this all the time,' he said, in his heavily accented English. 'The Adam's apple causes great unhappiness to these girls. To reduce it is a simple change that has a huge effect on the psychology. They come to me and they are wearing the scarves, and then a few weeks later the scarves are gone. They stand up straight and walk out in the street feeling happy. They are looking like who they feel they really are.' He returned to Milly. 'Now, you are lucky because your face is young and beautiful. Your bone structure is fine. Hmm, yes,' he said, taking her chin gently in hand and moving her face first one way, then the other. 'You look like your mother.' Oh, Dr van den Berg, you old flatterer. I wondered what was coming. 'Many of my girls', he continued, 'have other surgeries done. Take a look at these photos; here, you can see. Look, this girl has the brow reduction. The male brow has a ridge. I can remove this frontal bossing. Yours, I think, is not a problem, but if you like I can reduce it.'

'Sorry, what?' I interrupted. 'How?'

'I make an incision across the top of the scalp and carefully peel down the face from the skull, then I use a machine to grind down the brow ridge. Pull up the face again. Stitch, stitch, stitch and we are finished. All lovely and the scar is invisible; all in the hair.'

Oh, Milly, no, no, no. Please don't let anyone peel your face off. This was too much for me. I looked at her and she shook her head. 'I think I'm fine with the shape of my face,' she said. I breathed again.

'I agree with you,' said Dr van den Berg. 'I merely try to let you know your options. See here, the cheeks of this young lady before and after? I can raise the bone structure, better than just implants for sure. But you definitely don't need the cheek contouring. Very nice cheekbones. Perfect example.'

To my relief, we escaped the appointment without signing up for any further facial surgeries, and Milly now had a date for the tracheal shave in her diary for a couple of months' time. She would need various tests first and time to adjust her hormone levels to make the general anaesthesia safe, but once again she was ecstatic. Another piece of her elusive jigsaw puzzle was now in place.

Milly's Adam's apple anxiety and my encounter with Dr van den Berg had opened my eyes to a whole new level of physical alteration to which many trans women submit in the pursuit of a body that matches their inviolable sense of gender or in order to ease their dysphoria. If I had thought about it in the days of my ignorance, I suppose I would have divided trans women into those who simply dressed like women and those who had gone a step further and had genital surgery. Thanks to my long-ago reading of *Conundrum* I might have also remembered something about hormones, without really understanding the essential significance of that step. And until recently that had been the extent of my knowledge. I had come a very long way in the past two years, but this new information, the possibility of (or perceived need for) facial feminisation, was a revelation to me. Once I'd become alert to it, of course I could understand that the Adam's apple was a give-away, but frontal bossing and cheekbones? I may have thought these were plastic surgery issues designed to make someone more conventionally attractive, but I certainly hadn't realised that masculinity was bred in the bone in this way.

Tracheal shave surgery is, in fact, after sex reassignment surgery, the most common surgical alteration undergone by trans women. But after that tweak, the next area that comes under scrutiny is the top third of the face. The shape of the forehead is one of the most telling differences between males and females, with men typically having lower eyebrows and larger, wider eye sockets (the orbital ridge) in addition to the frontal bossing or brow ridge. Men's noses are also larger, longer and broader in relation to the size of their faces, their cheekbones have less forward projection and the chin is wider and squarer than women's. For a trans woman with pronounced masculine facial features, there is potentially much work that can be done to ameliorate these signs, and this type of surgery has become a new domain for maxillofacial and plastic surgeons. Bone can either be ground down or shaved away (on the forehead, nose and chin) or be built up with resin (on the cheekbones and eye sockets). Cheeks can be rounded out with implants or with fat harvested from other parts of the body, and lips can be lifted slightly to create a more characteristic feminine contour.

Needless to say, none of this comes cheap, and one of the cruelties of those who mock a trans woman for looking like a man in a dress is that her unconvincing looks are more likely due to being poor than oblivious. Most trans women whose faces do not 'pass' in a way society deems acceptable already suffer the pain of their own self-loathing, and most will despair at their features on a daily basis. Milly was fortunate in that her youthful transition meant the testosterone had not yet fully masculinised her face, and her genes gave her a naturally fine bone structure. I was relieved, though, to know that she herself did not feel the need for these procedures, and that the consultant, after a brief attempt to seduce her with his photo album, in fact agreed. Milly had blossomed into a beautiful young woman and

I hoped that the tracheal shave would mean an end to her anxieties about presenting in public, even though I knew her gender dysphoria would only ultimately be satisfied by sex reassignment surgery. Until that day came, I thought that by dealing with her Adam's apple she might at least find a measure of self-acceptance.

The days and weeks leading up to the trip to Belgium for Milly's surgery were busy for both of us. I was occupied with practice and organisation for an upcoming tour, and alongside her work Milly had numerous doctor's appointments to monitor the controlled lowering of her hormone dosage, so that she could minimise the risk of blood clots during and after the operation. The change in her hormone levels made her grumpy, irritable, restless and depressed; she was effectively going through something equivalent to premenstrual syndrome as her oestrogen and progesterone levels plunged. The hormonal mood swings were balanced by the new and tangible hope she felt at her imminent surgery. Milly was very excited but also very stressed. Recent travel experiences had been difficult and upsetting for Milly as her frequent travelling meant she had not been able to relinquish her passport to change her name, and her face began less and less to resemble someone who might conceivably be called Miles Martin. Milly never knew which way border control officials would view her and it caused her great anxiety. Would they address her as madam or sir? Would they look askance at her

or ask awkward questions in front of a queue of onlookers, onlookers who may be hostile? Her fears were
well-founded: on the Berlin trip, she had been arrested
and interrogated at the airport, accused of travelling on
a false passport.

Milly's anxiety was so bad that she felt she needed
someone with her when she travelled, and for a couple
of days afterwards as she recovered from the operation.
I agreed with her, but I was scheduled to be working in
France at the time, and this series of classes and concerts was not something that I could engage cover for.
Much as I wanted to, I couldn't go to Brussels. Edwards
and Dawson came to the rescue once again, and this
time there was an air of festivity about the enterprise.
The car was duly booked onto the Shuttle and a holiday apartment found, Milly's old banger was serviced,
and the boys dutifully gathered up the hazard warning
triangle, headlight deflectors, hi-vis vests and other
must-haves for their drive through Europe. Dawson
was put on the car insurance, vegan snacks were packed
and bottles of water stacked in the boot. Milly, Edwards and Dawson were going on a road trip, and I was
quietly delighted to see their excitement and Milly's
own optimism as she embarked on this new stage of
her journey. I was a nervous wreck, of course, terrified
at the thought of the surgery, no matter how relatively
trivial it might be; worried at the idea of my daughter
heading to an unknown clinic in a foreign city, flanked

by two incongruously adorable metalheads; anxious that I wouldn't be home to see her and make sure all was well when she got back from Belgium. And most of all, I sensed another moment of finality in this physical change. 'Goodbye!' I called brightly as they drove away. I couldn't let any of these feelings show. I was Milly's cheerleader come what may, and it was all going to be fine. 'Safe travels. Good luck!' I waved as the car turned out of the village lane, heading for the Channel, and went inside to cry a little bit.

By the next afternoon, I too was far away from Little Heywick and, in spite of the associated pressures of the moment, very happy to be back in France with the other two members of our trio. The next two weeks would be incessant, but we were all feeling rather in the holiday spirit as we enjoyed a late lunch and a glass of champagne at the end of our long journey. The next day students would arrive and we would need to teach and rehearse, as well as prepare for several concerts. It was all to be looked forward to, but in spite of that I struggled with anxiety knowing that Milly would soon be under a general anaesthetic and Dr van den Berg's expert knife. It was not easy balancing my private worries with the professional stresses of the event, although I was well used to both of them, but I did my best to hide my restlessness from my colleagues.

Milly rang me that evening to tell me that so far all was going according to plan. 'We got here,' she said, sounding excited. 'The car was fine; the apartment is nice. Edwards and Dawson took me to the clinic today for the pre-admission appointment and I saw Dr van den Berg again. He says everything is good, blood tests, health checks, all as it needs to be.'

'Are you feeling nervous?' I asked.

'So, so nervous, but still I can hardly wait. It's incredible to think that by tomorrow night this lump, this… thing, will be gone. The doctor said he'll do the tracheal shave through a small incision in the fold of the neck below the chin, then that will be sutured up and there'll be a small dressing on it. I'll be on pain medication, anti-inflammatories and antibiotics at first, and I'll have a swollen neck for a few weeks and a sore throat for the first few days. But as long as I do what I'm meant to do and take care of it properly, I should be back to normal in two weeks. I won't have to wear a scarf any more. I can't believe it's finally happening.' Another huge turning point was clearly on Milly's horizon and her excitement was palpable.

'Please ask Edwards and Dawson to call me when it's all over,' I said. There was nothing else I could do except wait for news tomorrow.

I was glad that the next day was very busy. My schedule didn't leave much time for worrying, but as the day went on I began to check my phone incessantly. It was evening before I heard from the boys, when I came off stage to find a text waiting for me. They were typically brief, and as usual focused on the important things. 'All done. Hard to get vegan food,' it read. 'Went to the gym. Milly OK. Going to play some guitar later.' Priorities, priorities: it seemed that practice would continue uninterrupted. I could only laugh, but in a private moment later that night I found myself trembling in secret relief at the knowledge that another step had been navigated unscathed. And then it occurred to me that there was only one thing left on the list. I still found it hard to contemplate, but Milly's next rite of passage would be the ultimate one. I had shied away from even thinking about what that would entail during all this time, but I knew now that it would probably not be long before the subject of sex reassignment surgery reared its head. I lay there in the dark, staring at the dusty hotel chandelier. I knew that soon I would, yet again, be adrift in uncharted waters. I needed to prepare myself.

CHAPTER 16

It was a relief to have a month or two of relative quiet once Milly and I were home again. My next trip was several months away, and I was happy to have some downtime so that I could start preparing the house for sale. I had decided that I needed to move on after Baz's death. Living surrounded by his personal effects and all the memories that were embedded in the very fabric of the home we had built together did not bring me any comfort, and I wanted a fresh start. It was a big job. Baz had been a great collector of things and had left a workshop full of half-completed projects. There were old clocks and musical boxes, a junk-shop worth of antiques waiting to be restored, model boats that would never be built. An unfinished harpsichord. Fishing gear, scrap metal, fine veneers for woodworking and endless mysterious items that came under the category of 'might be useful one day'. His magpie tendencies were very much at odds with my own minimalist style, and it was time for it all to go. The process of clearing everything was gruelling and exhausting, and yet also strangely soothing. As load after load went to family, friends, charity and the tip, I felt myself becoming lighter and freer, and I sensed that this newly open vista was creating the mental and physical space I needed to find a way forward in my changing world. No change was greater, of course, than my chameleon-like relationship with Milly. Every new step she took required a mental recalibration, an attempt to define the new 'normal', and I lived with a constant sense of imbalance as I tried to find my feet in the quicksand.

Milly was very caught up with a stream of gigs and recording sessions, which left time for little else. The transformation in her confidence since the Adam's apple surgery was remarkable, and as she blossomed, so did her career. Just as Dr van den Berg had predicted, she had thrown away the scarves and now walked tall, delighting in clothes that not only exposed her throat but drew attention to her slender neck. She radiated happiness and poise. In every outward appearance, Milly looked like the woman she wanted to be, but although for many trans women this is enough, I knew it never had been for Milly. She was still on the waiting list for the Charing Cross Gender Identity Clinic, although the prospect of surgery on the NHS remained all but invisible in the distance. The long-awaited first appointment at the GIC, when she finally went, was with a psychiatrist, and the meeting left Milly angry and disappointed. The consultant gave no quarter to the progress Milly had already made in her presentation or on the hormone therapy, and instead insisted that she stop taking the drugs until her second psychiatric appointment in a year's time. It was only at that second appointment that she could be formally diagnosed with the gender identity disorder which would trigger the medical stages of her treatment. The fact that that ship had clearly sailed long ago made not a jot of difference. Those were the rules. She would, they said, have to wait at least six years for surgery. Milly was furious at the intractable position shown by her doctors but was lucky that, in the background, Dr Thompson remained supportive and willing to keep working with Professor Frost, whatever the rule-bound GIC might say. Milly's prescriptions continued, though not before many desperate pleas were made, and she was frustrated and affronted by the slow-moving official process in which she seemed to be irrevocably entangled.

Although the tracheal shave surgery had made a striking difference to Milly's happiness, after a while an air of hopelessness started to seep back into her demeanour. I had come to realise there was a pattern in Milly's response to the changes she was bringing about in her own life. First, there would be a sinking depression as she grappled with whatever aspect of her dysphoria currently afflicted her, and then a period of agitation as she gathered the courage to talk about it. Next, there was anticipation and hope as she researched what she could do to take another step forward, a time when she would talk to me for hours about her thoughts and options. Excitement and optimism would build and then, as she ventured that step, there would be huge anxiety before she confronted her fears, which she did with great courage. A golden period of lightness and delight would follow. And then would come the crash. There was always the next thing, another step. Her journey would never be finished until she was finally freed of the loathsome body that she had been born with.

So when that conversation did arrive, I knew it was coming. All the signs were there. After a few months in a haze of happiness, Milly had started to become despondent. The house clearing provided a distraction, for me at least, and we sat together on the floor of the music studio going through boxes of old papers that had been stored in the loft. 'I can't believe he kept all this rubbish,' I said. 'It's crazy. Look… an electricity bill from 1986. Bin. And this, July 1979, "Dear Sir, please find herewith the harp strings you ordered…" Bin.'

'Mum…'

'This envelope is full of train tickets from 1992. Good grief, what was he thinking? Bin.'

'Mum, I need to talk to you,' Milly said.

'I thought so,' I replied.

'I've done everything I can with the GIC. I'm still a year away from being diagnosed with gender identity disorder, and maybe another two years away from the first NHS endocrinology appointment, maybe more. And then I have to prove that I've been living in my new gender role on the hormones for another twelve months, in spite of the fact that I will have already been doing that for years by then. And only at that point will they have a team meeting to decide whether I can be referred for sex reassignment surgery. I feel like it's never going to end. It's one hoop after another, constantly trying to please the gatekeepers. I can't live like this, not knowing when, or even if, I'll ever have the surgery.'

'But what other option is there?' Into the bin went a copy of Uncle Harry's will, circa 1985.

'The only alternative is to have it done privately. I've been looking into it.' I had no doubt this was the case.

'But what about the cost, Milly?' I said. 'It would be a fortune. How can you possibly afford it?'

'I can't. But I'll find a way. I'll borrow the money. There has to be a way for me.'

With every word, the impossible seemed to come closer into view and I struggled as I tried to measure my words and find a callow middle way between support and dissuasion. Inside, I was consumed by my own battle against what now appeared to be the inevitable. 'I can't bear the thought of what you would be doing to your body. The surgery, the risks… I can't even think about it. I know how important it is to you, but I don't know how I'll ever get there. I hate the thought of hospitals and surgery anyway, but something so drastic just because you…'

Hurt flashed across Milly's face. 'You don't know anything about it,' she said angrily. 'You think you do, but you don't. If I had a terminal disease that could be fixed with surgery but the waiting list was so long you knew I might die before I could have it, wouldn't you do anything to help?'

'Well, yes,' I said. 'Of course I would. It goes without saying. If private treatment would save you in a situation like that, of course I'd do whatever I could. But that's not a fair comparison. As hard as it is for me to say this to you, this is just something you want. It's mental, not physical.'

'It *is* a physical disorder,' she shouted, fury flooding her cheeks. 'And if the only way forward for me is to get a bank loan to pay for the surgery, then that is what I am going to do.' If there was one thing I could always be sure of with Milly it was that she would have done her research, and it was uncomfortable to realise that I might have let my own fears distort my knowledge and understanding of the true basis of my daughter's condition. Milly was right; if I would be prepared in other circumstances to help her have the best and quickest treatment for any other serious illness, and if this genuinely was a physical disorder of sorts, then my position was starkly inconsistent. I owed it to her to educate myself not just on the external manifestations of being transgender, as I had done, but, as far as I could, on the medical science behind it too. Was it psychological or physiological? Did anyone really know? And did it make a difference anyway?

What I learnt was that scientific opinion is, in fact, quite divided on the subject, although increasingly it is leaning strongly towards accepting that transgenderism originates in the structure and chemistry of the brain. So much so that in 2019 the World Health Organization removed sexual incongruence (its term for those whose gender identity does not match the gender assigned at birth) from the category of mental disorders and into a category relating to physical sexual health. 'We now have a better understanding that this isn't actually a mental health condition,' their spokesman announced. New techniques such as functional magnetic resonance imaging (fMRI) have exposed the similarities and differences between the brains of trans- and cisgender people which may explain the inner conviction that trans individuals feel of a gender at variance with their natal sex.

One of the most prominent hypotheses for gender dysphoria is that sexual differentiation of the genitals occurs separately from sexual differentiation of the brain structure in the womb, making it possible that the mind and body can at times diverge on this fundamental issue.

The implication of this, of course, is that gender, and not just biological sex, is determined before birth, a position profoundly at odds with arguments for the social construction of gender so important in the past fifty years of feminist theory. Nonetheless, sex differences in the brain are now well documented, and though it remains contested whether the origins of these are biological or social, the idea that a developmental mismatch between gender and sex can arise *in utero* is supported by a number of studies. In particular, it seems that hormonal exposure in the womb may have an effect, and I found this fascinating. Could my pre-natal certainty that my child was a girl have been because that foetus was exposed to the 'wrong' hormones, or, conversely I suppose, that my baby was gendered female because my body had sent the wrong messages and that somehow, on a deep, intuitive level, I knew this?

As long ago as the 1990s, a pioneering study by Professor Dick Swaab involving post-mortem examination of the brains of transgender women at the Netherlands Institute for Neuroscience found that parts of the brains of trans women (the central subdivision of the bed nucleus of the stria terminalis, for the scientifically inclined) more closely resemble those of cisgender women than those of their natal sex. Importantly, this is a centre of the brain that is known to play a key role in sexual behaviour. Other studies have made similar findings regarding the hypothalamus, another region of the brain linked to sexual orientation. The extensive neuroimaging research of Stanford professor Robert Sapolsky confirms these findings and in his 2013 article 'Caught Between Male and Female', he concludes that there is a neurobiological explanation for cross-gender identification. In 2014, Georg Kranz, a neuroscientist at the Medical University of Vienna (hardly a bastion of wokeness, with a serious and esteemed history dating back to 1365), used diffusion MRI data to investigate differences in the microstructure of the brains of trans- and cisgendered women. The findings of Kranz's study showed that white matter microstructures in the brain are shaped by the hormonal environment before and soon after birth, and Kranz concluded that

all available evidence points towards a biologically determined identity. In [transgender] people you would say there was a mismatch in the testosterone milieu during the development of the body and then during the development of the brain, so that the body was masculinised and the brain was feminised, or the other way around.

It would be intellectually dishonest, though, if I did not also acknowledge that there are other scientists who take a different position on the research, claiming that various studies are compromised by their small sample size, or that they are not properly controlled for psychological or social factors, or that the data is conflicting or inconclusive. I do not have the expertise to argue for or against the science and, like so much in life, I imagine the truth is that there are many complex factors at play. But, as with so much on this transgender journey, I have in the end had to come to my own conclusions, and they are, as before, that ultimately I don't need science or history or anthropology to validate my experience of my child, her suffering, and her determination to become what she feels she truly is. If studies that support a neurobiological cause of transgenderism give strength to the argument that trans people should be treated with empathy, dignity and understanding and receive the treatment they so desperately desire, then I am on the side of that science. If those studies remove the freakish stigma attached to transgenderism, giving trans people an explanation for their anguish and validating its medical solution, I gratefully accept them. And in any case, these days even the World Health Organization is on my side, and who am I to disagree with them? I now understood why Milly felt so passionately that her need for sex reassignment surgery was a physical imperative as well as an emotional one, and, though I still found the brutal thought of it hard to contemplate, I knew that I had no choice. As ever, my support would lie with my daughter, however hard the road ahead might be.

While I had been coming to terms with this new

dimension of my daughter's life, she, with Leigh's help, had been busy researching her options for private sex reassignment surgery. Whether on the NHS or privately, Milly had decided that she did not want to have the operation in the UK. The anecdotal evidence from discussion forums was that methods and results were generally not as good or as detailed in Britain. There is generally a great deal of dissatisfaction with surgical outcomes in the UK, where an operation that takes around four hours anywhere else is usually done and dusted in two hours or less. One might say that artistry is sacrificed for efficiency. The leading clinics were in California, Montreal and Bangkok, and Milly investigated all of them. The costs varied widely, but, more importantly, so did surgical style and reputation. How do you choose? Apparently (though I preferred not to participate in this part of the investigation) clinics freely display photographs of their surgeons' handiwork online, so that reconfigured genitals can be compared, discussed and ranked at leisure, to help you choose. Apart from aesthetics, the key attributes that Milly, like other trans women, sought – and of course this is not surprising if you think about it – were sensation and depth. Milly dismissed the Californian clinics, which some reported had a conveyor-belt approach to surgery, on the basis that if she was to put herself through a frankly terrifying experience, she wanted a surgeon with a kindly bedside manner who might take the time to

reassure her and provide aftercare. For similar reasons,
Montreal was discarded. The leading surgeon there was
a front-runner in the aesthetics department, and Milly
avidly studied his success stories on YouTube (for the
trans community, YouTube is an information resource
the equivalent of the British Library or the Library of
Congress), but some complained of lack of sensation
after surgery in Montreal. Though Milly was quick to
point out that 'the results really do look amazing'.

Two of the front-runners having been thus eliminated,
the choice was made. Milly would have her surgery in
Thailand. In fact, Thailand is the world centre for transgender surgery, and most of the world's leading surgeons
in the field have done their specialist training there, at
the Preecha Aesthetic Institute in Bangkok. Dr Preecha
Tiewtranon is a pioneer of gender change surgery and has
performed more than 3,500 operations over the past forty
years. He developed the revolutionary surgical techniques
now used around the world, and his institute is renowned
for its training. For Milly, like so many others, Thailand
offered an affordable, easily accessible, high-quality solution to her problem. So now the question was not where,
but who. In Thailand there are over 100 plastic surgeons
and urologists specialising in sex reassignment surgery
and at least twenty clinics performing the operations.
Transgender medical tourism is quite a niche market in
Bangkok, with around 90 per cent of patients coming
from Europe, Australia, the United States, China and the

Middle East. More weeks of research finally narrowed the field down to two: Dr Sarapong and Dr Soong, who had both been trained by Dr Preecha. The two surgeons use slightly different techniques and although Dr Soong's method gives outstanding results, a higher rate of complications has been reported and there is a much longer recovery time. Dr Sarapong is renowned for surgery that results in good sensation and depth with excellent aesthetic results. And so, the final choice was made, and with a stomach-churning mix of trepidation (me) and excitement (her) Milly contacted the Sarapong Clinic in Bangkok.

My concerns that Bangkok might be some kind of medical Wild West, a quick trip-and-snip destination ungoverned by international guidelines for best practice in trans surgery, were completely unfounded. The prerequisites for Milly's surgery were exactly the same as they would be anywhere else, and she began to piece together the preliminary documentation required under the international protocols. She could already document the real-life experience and hormone therapy, but now she had to provide three independent psychiatric evaluations. Milly had been so disheartened by her experience of the first Gender Identity Clinic psychiatrist that she begged Dr Thompson to refer her instead to a local psychiatrist to discuss the first appraisal. The appointment was months in coming, but when she arrived at the hospital this consultant did not take any convincing.

'Well, you look like you are certainly committed to your choice,' he said, taking in her feminine presentation at a glance. 'Can you confirm that this is what you really want?' They chatted for a short while and, there and then, the doctor wrote his letter of agreement. Milly had been formally diagnosed with gender identity disorder. She flew out of the building and, overcome with emotion, rang me: 'I've got it, I've got it,' she bubbled. 'Two more letters and everything is done.' The first letter was submitted to Dr Sarapong's clinic, and a rather more relaxed approach was taken to the next official sign-off. The clinic recommended an American psychiatrist in the Philippines who, for a couple of hundred dollars, would offer an online appointment and provide the necessary document. Properly qualified, all legitimate. It sounded a bit dubious to me, and even Milly agreed, but at least it was quick and easy. The final psychiatric assessment, which had to be made by a Thai psychiatrist, would happen at the clinic in the days before the operation. All the pieces were now in place, the money was found for the deposit and at last Milly had a date for the surgery that would finally change her life.

CHAPTER 17

I remembered my father's bewildered enquiry eighteen months earlier as to whether the final stage of transition would be that Milly's penis was cut off, and how I replied rather vaguely that I had heard it was somehow 'repurposed'. My knowledge then of what sex reassignment surgery involved was sketchy to say the least and, at that stage, that was how I liked it. There was only so much I could take on board in those early days. The horrifying idea of surgery (horrifying to me, at least) seemed a distant prospect back then, and I was quite happy to allow a discreet veil to fall over the technicalities. But now, with the surgery just six months away, and knowing that Leigh, who was now a permanent fixture in Milly's life, and I would share the burden of support and aftercare, I decided that I needed to know more. I would learn what was about to happen to my child's body.

What I read left me full of admiration and astonishment. Male-to-female sex reassignment surgery is actually a complex suite of surgeries undertaken during one long operation (usually around four hours), known by the overarching term of penile inversion vaginoplasty. The end result is that the male sex organs are partially removed and reconfigured to create a sensitive and aesthetically pleasing simulacrum of genetically female sex organs. More than one person I have talked to about my daughter's surgery has asked in amazement, 'So, can she have a baby?', which I have to say has greatly surprised me. These specialists can certainly do remarkable things, but a full working transplant of the womb, fallopian tubes and ovaries is not among them, although, of course, who knows what the future may hold?

Styles and techniques vary from surgeon to surgeon but the fundamentals remain the same. The testes are removed (this part of the operation is known as orchiectomy), but the scrotal skin and all its nerve endings are kept intact and used to create the inner and outer labia. The penis is dissected and the erectile tissue fully removed (a partial penectomy), and an opening which will become the vagina is made in the perineum. The glans, nerves and blood vessels are carefully separated from the penile shaft, and the skin of the penis is inverted and pulled back to line the new vaginal cavity. The glans of the penis remains attached to its nerves and is reshaped and repositioned to form a clitoris, and the urethra is shortened and its opening relocated to the usual female position. Unsurprisingly, this level of surgery is not without its risks and complications, so much so that revision is frequently required later (and indeed some surgeons, Dr Sarapong included, offer a kind of two-for-one guarantee, where, if there are later problems, they are remedied for free). The depth of the vagina varies according to how much penile skin is available to create it, but a good result will give around six or seven inches with full sensation. In short, by the end of the procedure and once healed, a trans woman can look forward to the full complement of sensate female genitalia that, if done well, are visually and functionally indistinguishable from those of cisgendered women.

As the date of the surgery approached, Milly became increasingly anxious and retreated into an almost trance-like state in which she survived daily life on autopilot. I was desperately worried for her during those days, but in every conversation we had where I questioned her repeatedly, 'Are you sure?', she gave the same answer: 'I've never been more sure of anything.' Later I asked her if, during this time, she had ever considered cancelling (so close had I thought she was to it). She replied, 'Not even for a single moment.' No matter how great her terror, and it was absolute, this change was her last and final attempt at a life worth living, and she would take it, no matter what the outcome, no matter what the fear. I was, as ever, humbled by her courage. I have always tried to be strong in the face of life's challenges, but the obstacles I have faced pale into insignificance beside my daughter's experience. As a parent, it is a fascinating and instructive process to learn from your own children, to navigate that sea change in the status quo where you are no longer their guide and teacher but their companion and sometimes even their student.

All the arrangements were now in place. Flights had been booked and an apartment found in Bangkok for the five weeks before and after the surgery and related appointments. Milly had cleared her work schedule to give herself a three-month period of recuperation once she was home again. Practising and performing at professional level is a physically strenuous activity no matter what your instrument, and Milly was realistic about the time it would take before she would be properly back on her feet, able to work the long hours required, perform on stage and carry her heavy instruments and gear. Leigh was flying over from Connecticut and travelling to Thailand with Milly from London, and Leigh's father, Mike, had also joined the enterprise. The plan was that he would spend the first three weeks with Milly and Leigh in Bangkok, then we would change shifts and I would fly out for the remaining two weeks. I was grateful to Mike for his support; if I had been squeamish about the Adam's apple surgery, it was as nothing compared to my feelings about the operation ahead. I was aware of my own limitations: I couldn't cope with the thought of watching my daughter being wheeled away for this frightening surgical metamorphosis, and I was worried that my fear would infect her. I knew that I would be much more use on Team Recovery.

The cold January morning that I drove Milly and Leigh to London Heathrow is seared in my memory. The atmosphere in the car was febrile. Leigh was bouncy and excited; Milly was by turn snappy and catatonic; and I was sick to my stomach with anxiety. A thin veneer of normality overlaid the pervasive uneasiness, and I filled the vast and empty expanse of the unknown that lay between us with trivial questions and advice. 'Have you packed the sunscreen? Do you have enough T-shirts? It will be hot. Make sure you only drink bottled water. Don't eat salad you haven't washed yourself.' Like any mother taking her daughter and girlfriend to the airport as they headed off on their tropical adventure. And then, it was time. Check in, coffee and we were at the gate. Milly hugged me, was gone, and I was bereft in the space she left behind her. There was nothing more to do but drive home and wait to hear from them.

Milly and Leigh called me on Skype the next day. They were installed in their apartment, tired, hot and jet-lagged. Mike was there and Milly had already had her first pre-operative consultation at the clinic. 'It was fine,' she said. 'Everyone was so kind to me. We had to wait hours to be seen and the consulting rooms are shabbier than I expected, but once I talked to Dr Sarapong I felt really reassured. He went through the risks, but there was nothing I didn't already know.'

'What happens next?' I asked. 'How are you feeling?'

'Scared,' said Milly, 'but optimistic. Incredibly nervous. Excited. We've got a free day tomorrow to rest, then the next day they're sending a driver to take us to Bangkok hospital for blood tests, HIV test, that kind of thing. And the final psychiatric appointment. Then twenty-four hours fasting, and then that's it. It finally happens.'

Four days from now it would all be over. Well, the worst of it. Things could only get better after this, I supposed, though I doubted that the recovery would be easy either. It was, after all, very major surgery. I was wracked with anxiety, and my friend organised a rehearsal of our trio for the day of the operation to take my mind off things. I think none of us really expected much effective practising to be done that day. I knew it was just a way of surrounding me with support when I most needed it, and I was deeply grateful both for that care and for the distraction.

We started the rehearsal early when the day came, but in Thailand it was already mid-afternoon. Bach, Galli and Briccialdi filled the music room, along with the usual banter and teasing, but a part of my mind was elsewhere, and every time my phone rang or pinged with an alert I leapt up to check it. Nothing yet. It wasn't until nearly lunchtime that I finally heard from Leigh, and even then there was no real news. It had been a long day. Dr Sarapong was delayed and Milly had only just been taken down to the operating theatre, but now she was on her way. I drew a deep breath, feeling like I might faint at any moment, and leaned shakily against the piano. 'Let's keep playing,' I said. I needed to retreat into the music until I heard from Leigh that Milly was back, awake. Reborn.

The stress of waiting for that call was immense, and when I finally heard my FaceTime ringtone nearly eight hours later the adrenaline surged and I gasped, my heart pounding. This was it. Please let it be alright. Leigh waved at me from the screen of my phone, 'She's back! She's awake. Well, not really awake. Off her head on pethidine, but drifting in and out. Look, here she is.' Leigh moved her laptop around and I caught a glimpse of the hospital room and then of Milly, half asleep and strumming a travel-sized acoustic guitar. Some things never change.

'Mum,' she said weakly. She was hooked up to drips and drains, covered lightly with a sheet with a pillow under her knees, and propped up slightly on the raised end of the bed. 'It hurts so much.' Her face was covered with a sheen of sweat and her eyes were half-closed.

'Oh, Milly.'

'The transfer board was covered in so much blood when they lifted her off the trolley,' Leigh said. Not really the kind of thing I was hoping to hear, but at least I knew, I suppose.

'I'm in so much pain,' Milly sobbed. 'But I'm so happy. I'm so happy. Ecstatic, I'm just...' She petered out, drained by the effort and overcome by emotion.

It was enough. 'Just sleep now. Thank you so, so much, Leigh. You should get some rest too.'

'I'm sleeping here in the room,' Leigh said. 'This hospital is amazing. There's a chaise longue for me and a little kitchen area and a lovely bathroom. Very five-star! I'm going to stay with Milly for as long as she needs it. I'll call you tomorrow.'

'Or before then, if anything goes wrong...'

'There's nothing to go wrong now. It's over,' Leigh said. 'Milly's going to be fine.'

That evening, I drove home across the English countryside, avoiding the motorways for a quieter route where I could finally let the unremitting tension of the day go. I was hugely relieved but exhausted, too. I knew there was much still to come as Milly made her recovery, but I would be there for that, and for now I knew my daughter was safe, and that was the main thing. Tonight I would sleep, and perhaps, I mused, tomorrow I might see her again, maybe sitting up a little more, maybe looking a little stronger, maybe able to speak to me and tell me how it was. To tell me it was all worthwhile.

Milly was in hospital for five days after the surgery and for most of that time she was in severe pain, relieved only by constant infusions of pethidine given through her drip. I relied on Leigh for every update and, when I got them, they were always an unsettling combination of happiness and horror. The details unfolded gradually as Leigh herself struggled with the brutality of Milly's post-operative condition. Milly was right in not wanting me there for the surgery; Leigh has a background in biological sciences and was much better equipped than I to deal with this. I had had more than enough of hospitals for one lifetime with Baz's illness and death, and have always turned queasily away from even the smallest exposure to bodily wounds. I would have been useless. On the third day, the nurses encouraged Milly to attempt to stand and take a few steps, and Leigh rang to tell me the news. 'She's up, sort of, attached to her drip and the bags and drains, but still, up,' Leigh said happily. 'She walked from the bed to the edge of the room, leaning on the nurses. It was agony though. They gave her pethidine again at the end of it. It's so strange – every time she has pethidine she starts crying. She's wiped out now, but it's definitely progress.' Day by day Milly was feeling stronger and becoming more comfortable, and on day five it was time for the dressings, packing, drains and stent to be removed. Milly was leaving the hospital.

Dr Sarapong arrived to take care of the unveiling,

and it was the first time Milly had seen her transformation. It was both wonderful and horrifying. 'There are so many stitches,' she told me when we spoke later that day. 'So much blood, so much swelling. It's just a big, mangled, bruised, bloody mess.'

'It's what I was expecting,' Leigh reassured me. 'It's an extensive surgical wound, but it's all healthy. No dead tissue, no infection. It doesn't look great right now, but Dr Sarapong said the healing process will take months and that it's all good.'

'I'm confident,' said Milly, although she didn't sound terribly confident to me. 'Ever since the surgery I've been so scared about what I'd see. I didn't know what it would be like when the dressings came off, but now I'm feeling calm. I just need time to heal. They've given me a rubber ring to sit on,' she added. 'I'm a bit worried about the car ride home this afternoon. I haven't sat up for very long yet, and the traffic here is a nightmare so it could take hours.'

Milly was sent home with two lots of antibiotics, two different types of painkillers, some Xanax to help her sleep and a follow-up appointment at the clinic for a few days' time. Walking was incredibly painful, and she was so incapacitated that Mike purchased a wheelchair for her from the hospital. It's important to say here that some people leap up joyfully from their transition surgery, able to head out on gentle shopping trips and tourist excursions within a week or two. This most certainly was not the case for Milly. Although in many ways Dr Sarapong did a wonderful job, Milly was in acute pain for a long time, the cause of which was only diagnosed many months later. As far as I know, her long and painful recovery process is not typical, but, as always, I can only tell my own story, and the fact that revision surgery is so common I think validates that, as upsetting as it may be. It's a complex and significant surgical procedure, and things can and do go wrong. But in spite of the immediate pain and all the residual discomfort of the next few weeks and months, not once did Milly ever express the tiniest regret. She was quite simply overjoyed to have crossed the final barrier, and whatever difficulties came with it were trivial to her.

Leigh rang me when they arrived back at the apartment. 'The drive was terrible. We're only about five miles from the hospital and it took two and a half hours. Milly was on her rubber ring and she was in agony. She collapsed on the bed when we got in and she's sleeping now. The clinic appointment is in two days' time and they're sending a car for us again, so I'm just hoping that trip will be easier.' In fact, every day she was a bit better, and so when the day of the visit to Dr Sarapong's clinic came, she was looking forward to hearing his assessment of her results and finding out more about her progress. For a start, Milly knew that her drug regime would change now. She had stopped taking the cyproterone acetate tablets immediately after her surgery;

no more testicles meant no more testosterone, and she would never have to take anti-androgens again. But she had also been off the oestrogen for several weeks, due to the risk of blood clotting during surgery, and she was anxious to go back on them as soon as possible. She also knew that she would have to begin a routine of daily dilation to prevent the newly created vagina from closing and had been warned that this would be painful. At the clinic appointment, she would receive advice on all these changes, and after all the recent highs and lows she was quietly excited about this next step.

Milly and Leigh called me on Skype that evening. It had been another long day. As I would soon experience for myself, Dr Sarapong had many skills but timekeeping was not among them, and it was quite normal to have to wait four or five hours to be seen at his clinic. On one occasion when she was in hospital, Milly told me, he swept in with his entourage to examine her at three o'clock in the morning, and no one seemed to think it was in the least bit strange. Milly was rather bubbly tonight, the best I had seen her so far. It was now day seven, and she was definitely perking up. 'Dr Sarapong says it's all healing well,' she said happily. 'It still looks awful, but everything is where it should be. I can go back on the hormones once I get back to England. I need to stay off them for now because I'm not very mobile yet and I've got a long flight ahead, but I can start taking them again soon. And he taught me to dilate!'

'That was definitely weird,' Leigh interjected. I could well imagine it was.

'It was really painful, and there's not much depth yet because of the internal swelling, but Dr Sarapong said that will gradually subside. Oh, and at the end I got a little carry bag with a ribbon handle to take my new dilator home in.' There was something about that little detail of the pretty ribbon-tied bag that I found strangely moving. Among all the pain and impossible wonders, it was that kind and delicate detail that finally reduced me to tears.

CHAPTER 18

arrived at Bangkok Suvarnabhumi airport early in the morning and stepped out into a wall of humidity. Hot, tired from travelling and weighed down by a heavy suitcase, I thought I would take a taxi to the apartment in the Lumphini district of the city. I soon regretted this decision, although at least it gives me the opportunity to offer another observation from the frontline of my transgender journey: if visiting Bangkok for surgery (or indeed any reason), trust me, take the airport train. The city's public transport network is quick, clean, cheap and efficient, but that taxi ride took hours. And hours. I passed a little time entertaining myself with the signs along the freeway: 'Buddha decoration means NO respect. Don't buy or sell Buddha,' they read. 'Buddha is not for tattoo.' Noted. My Thailand visit was already quite exotic enough without venturing down that particular route. 'Save the environment, delete old data on your computer.' Really? That seemed like a remarkably feeble solution to global warming. I found myself briefly grateful for the distraction as my mind wrestled with how this might work. In spite of an address written in Thai, the driver had no idea how to find the side street where the apartment was located, and when at one point he took me completely off-grid to an abandoned building site, I started to worry. But he was just making a little personal detour; we had after all been driving for nearly three hours by this stage. A few minutes later, as we took to the road again, a torrential downpour stopped us, and all of the traffic, in our tracks, and I watched in amazement as pedestrians found themselves shin-deep in water and main roads turned into rivers. Coupled with the anxiety I was already feeling and the listless weariness born of thirteen hours in the air, none of this felt like an auspicious start to my visit. I was greatly relieved when the taxi driver, assisted by my increasingly desperate backseat attempts at navigating with my phone, finally approached a street corner with a name I recognised. I was nearly there.

'Stop,' I said, not wishing to spend another moment in the car, 'stop here. I walk. Walk,' I gestured, making little wiggling movements with my fingers.

The meter read just 300 baht, about £5, so at least I'd seen quite a lot of Bangkok for my money. I finally escaped the taxi and dragged my luggage along the still-sodden street, stepping cautiously around the flotsam, edging past rickety tables stacked high with vegetables and avoiding the spitting chicken parts frying on stoves along the footpath. A guard saluted me from his sentry box at the entrance to the building and I walked with relief into the cool, dark lobby.

The apartment complex was incongruous in its chaotic surroundings, quite obviously intended as the height of expensive luxury in its 1970s heyday. Now it was marooned amid a shambles of back alleys and small local markets. Perhaps there had been some greater vision for the area that had never materialised, but I rather liked it, with its air of faded glory holding on stubbornly in the midst of this traditional neighbourhood. Leigh came bouncing out to meet me, purple hair flying and tattoos (no Buddha) on display in her summery clothes, and we went up to the apartment together. It was enormous, with a wide expanse of polished wooden floor in the middle of which sat a wheelchair. 'It's big enough to race around,' Leigh laughed. 'Sometimes I do.' The decor was Asian chic circa 1976, and it had a shabby retro fabulousness about it. There were several Buddhas on shelves and side tables, which I can only assume were not for decoration. And then, after 6,000 miles and an unimaginable journey through suffering and fear, there was my daughter.

Milly was lying on the bed, propped up on a nest of pillows and surrounded by pills and paraphernalia. Dozens of bouquets of tropical flowers sent by Leigh's family (though not by Milly's) and from friends and colleagues across the world covered the floor and dressing table, spilling out into the dining room. She was weaker and more fragile than when I had last seen her, and the toll of the past couple of weeks was clearly etched on her face. I could see that she was struggling, wincing with pain as she moved to greet me, but she also looked radiantly happy. 'Mum,' she said quietly. I sat on the edge of the bed and held her as she buried her face in my shoulder. 'I love you.' And just like that, I knew it had all been worthwhile. No doubt I would hear more soon, and I expected all the stories of pain and joy to tumble out, but right now I just wanted to be there with her. With the daughter who I knew felt that she had finally achieved her real place in the world.

I had arrived at the apartment at the time when Milly was due to dilate and, as I would quickly learn, that stopped for nothing. Her dilation timetable would rule our days for the next couple of weeks (and Milly's for the rest of her life). As with anything Milly undertook, the schedule was rigidly adhered to. Dr Sarapong had advised that she needed to dilate three times a day for an hour at a time, and no matter how great the pain Milly did so. Imagine, if you can bear to, a wound sutured with over 200 stitches, still prone to bleeding, swollen, barely beginning to granulate; and then imagine that instead of tenderly covering it and letting it slowly heal, taking care of every movement, trying not to pull it, imagine that every day you had to plunge something deep into that wound and leave it there to prevent it from closing. And that you had to do it three times a day. Dilating is an agonising process, but essential. If the dilation routine is not properly followed, the new vaginal opening will close up along its length as the internal skin graft contracts and the body's natural healing mechanisms cause the raw skin to adhere and create scar tissue. Frequent dilation is the only way to prevent this happening, and for the first four months Milly dilated for three hours a day. As the swelling gradually reduced and the wounds healed, that was reduced to twice a day, and then a year later, if all went well (which for Milly it did not), to once a week. By this time it would no longer be painful, but proper dilation after surgery is a long and exacting experience. The process will always be an essential part of Milly's life. Once we were home again, Milly upgraded her single acrylic dilator to a more highly recommended set in graduated sizes and different colours, and I became used to seeing this rainbow collection lined up in the bathroom. In Bangkok, during those early days, though, dilation with the slim Sarapong model was the most she could manage, and this absolute priority was an ordeal that everything else revolved around. On several occasions it fell to me to walk through the rabbit warren of back alleys to a part of the city where there were Western-style pharmacies, in search of water-based lube for my daughter, and on those long walks I sometimes felt light-headed at the bizarre turn my life had taken.

Milly cried frequently as she began the fragile and painful process of healing in that Bangkok apartment. She cried often from happiness, often from pain, but I think mostly from a kind of post-operative trauma. Gradually, though, she felt strong enough to tell me more and more about what had happened in the hospital, and although I had had constant updates from Leigh at the time, some of what I now heard was new and distressing. More than once, as she grappled with her experiences, Milly talked about being taken to the operating theatre. Dr Sarapong had been late (again), and she lay waiting on the trolley for several hours. The anaesthetist visited and was kind and encouraging, but she felt abandoned there, missing Leigh's comforting presence. As the time passed, her fear grew, until finally she was consumed, as she put it to me, by a raw and visceral animal terror. She had moved beyond any rational thought and felt her mind and body retreat into a world of base instinctual response. When the nurses finally came to take her in to the theatre, fear had overtaken her. 'I was shaking uncontrollably,' she told me. 'Nothing could stop it, every muscle was trembling convulsively. They had to hold onto me as they wheeled me into the theatre, and then they put me on a cross-shaped table with my arms out to the side and strapped me down to stop me moving.' I was appalled. Not at the medical staff – Milly reassured me repeatedly that they were gentle, careful and considerate – but to hear first-hand of the frightening mental violence her ordeal had wrought on her. No wonder she needed time to cry and to regain her emotional balance.

As the latter days of our Bangkok sojourn approached, Milly started to gain in strength and gradually became more mobile. She still found it difficult to walk for more than a very short time but was determined to push herself to her limit. As part of that rehabilitation we went on occasional gentle outings to shopping malls where she browsed through pretty clothes, overjoyed at the thought that there would be no more tucking needed to wear them. Some days, if she was feeling well enough, she might even venture to try something on, a flowing skirt or a summer dress. Anything tight in the lower half was out of the question and would be for a while, and she needed clothes that would accommodate her new body comfortably. These outings were painful and slow, and we limped through department stores and indoor markets at a snail's pace. Leigh was endlessly patient, helping Milly with tenderness into dressing rooms, her arms full of clothes. I was less forbearing, I know; I walked too fast, I wandered off if I saw something that interested me. Milly's determination was almost more than I could bear to watch. She did not admit to it, but I saw the tension around her mouth and the tears that she would not let fall as she struggled to walk.

Sometimes, in the end, the pain got the better of her and she would collapse back into the wheelchair that we pushed around with us everywhere. I hated that wheelchair. I hated the thought that my strong, beautiful child was so broken that she was – at least for the present – disabled by what she had put her body through. I wrestled with this unspoken anguish while outwardly attempting to bounce enthusiastically through these expeditions. But when it was my turn to push the wheelchair, that inner turmoil played itself out as I propelled Milly through the crowds impatiently, carelessly bumping the chair. I've never claimed to be Florence Nightingale, but I know I was also too often insensitive to the pain that every small knock caused her. Sometimes I feel that being the mother of a trans child is an endless catalogue of errors and long-overdue apologies.

These post-op weeks in Bangkok were certainly no holiday, in spite of a suggestion on one clinic website that 'after the surgery, side trips can be enjoyed'. My days seemed mainly to involve finding food that my vegan daughter would eat (it was almost impossible to avoid nam pla, a fish sauce which pervades Thai cuisine), lugging home endless bottles of water, buying packets of sanitary towels and, of course, keeping the lube supply topped up. In an occasional stolen hour, I would wander around the back-street food stalls near the apartment, taking in the sights and smells, and delighting in the exotic fruit and vegetables. Dried fish hung from dusty awnings, and skewers of chicken roasted on braziers. Old ladies threaded marigolds and orchids into garlands, and children played in the gutter, by some magic their school uniforms remaining immaculate. It was hot and humid, and I would return to the apartment with my clothes and hair damp with perspiration, energised by the brief respite.

An appointment with Dr Sarapong was the final milestone in our Bangkok pilgrimage, after which Milly would be able to return to England. I was curious to see the clinic for myself, especially now that the worst was over and I did not have to confront the flesh and gore in my imagination, or, worse, actually experience it. As before, a driver was sent and we were chauffeured to the appointment in one of the clinic's fleet of air-conditioned Mercedes. At first, we drove slowly through the nose-to-tail traffic, along major thoroughfares lined with expensive international brands. Soon, though, our driver turned off into one of Bangkok's bewildering mazes of side streets, and we seemed to head further and further away from the kind of place one might expect to find a famous aesthetic surgery destination. The clinic, when we eventually arrived there, was on a gritty avenue of motorcycle spare parts dealers, interspersed with cosmetic clinics and masseurs. A pizza shop on one side, second-hand exhaust mufflers and reconditioned tyres on the other. It was far from what

I had been expecting, though the clinic itself was glossy and spotless, with staff as well-groomed as air hostesses. We waited, and waited, and waited, until night fell. Dr Sarapong's timekeeping had clearly not improved at all in the past month, and he had not yet even arrived from his day in the operating theatre. To pass the time I decided I would walk a little, and so I left Milly and Leigh alone and headed out along the road. Lights now hung from all the awnings and food of all sorts was cooking in shop fronts and over glowing coals in rusty oil drums. A canal intersected the road, running briefly underneath it through a small culvert. The water was dirty brown and strewn with rubbish, and the quiet banks of reeds and bamboo on either side were curiously at odds with the makeshift urban chaos around the canal. Barrows were piled with herbs and leafy vegetables and the aroma of charcoal mixed with the savoury steam that poured out of every doorway. Loud and incessant chatter filled the air, and plastic bins of ice overflowed with bottles of local beer. The cheerful hubbub lightened my mood and I pretended to myself that I was simply one more traveller on a south-east Asian holiday.

It was after eight o'clock when Milly was finally called into the consulting room. Leigh went with her, and I was grateful to be excused. Nothing can really prepare you for the idea that you are about to see your child's natal sex erased and recreated in a new body, and the thought was more than a little overwhelming. The results, though, when they were uncovered, were just as Leigh had told her: bruised and swollen, but without doubt beautifully female. Dr Sarapong carefully removed the external stitches, with words of advice and congratulations, and answered Milly's concerns about swelling, appearance and aftercare. And then it really was over. Milly was shaky but glowing, and Leigh never left her side, helping her to dress and supporting her with soothing words and gestures. The three of us walked out of the clinic to the waiting car and a driver took us back again through the unceasing traffic and pulsating nightlife of central Bangkok to the peace of our apartment.

'I hope I never have to come back,' said Milly.

'Why should you?' I asked.

'If I need more surgery. I won't be able to tell until all the swelling completely subsides, but if there are any problems then I might have to. It takes a year before you can know if it was a complete success.'

I had known that revision surgery was common, but still this came as a shock and a disappointment to me. The potential complications of vaginoplasty include vaginal prolapse, recurrent pain and bleeding, infections and narrowing of the urethra causing difficulties in urinating. There might also be loss of sensation or sexual function, or aesthetic dissatisfaction with the size or shape of the newly created clitoris or labia. In short, there were plenty of things that could still go wrong, and it would be quite a while before Milly would know if the end result was really as good as she hoped it might be.

Even so, tonight I wanted to celebrate. Although it was now very late, I walked a couple of miles through the back alleys, alight with fried chicken shacks and spitting braziers, towards a quarter of the city where I knew there was a Western-style supermarket. There, I managed to procure a chilled bottle of white wine of dubious provenance. Even though the teetotal Milly would only push the boat out with a sparkling water and a slice of lime, and the ever-supportive Leigh kept her company in this, for me that glass of wine would be a benediction on my own journey's end. As I sat on the balcony in the warm night air, glass in hand, at last I felt a sense of calm and release, and finally allowed in myself the birth of hope for this child of mine.

CHAPTER 19

And I'd like to finish my journey there, if I could.
Me, my daughter and the irrepressible Leigh happily sitting on that Bangkok balcony with a cold glass of wine, chatting and laughing, one lifetime behind us and a new one ahead. Ready to fly back to England in the morning, each of us full of anticipation for a happier future. Wouldn't that image round the story off perfectly? But it wasn't like that, as so often things are not. We did leave the next day and life did revert to normal, and it is true that it was a new and better kind of normal. In due course, Leigh went back to New Haven, Milly went back to work, and of course so did I. But those early months of Milly's recovery were far from easy. Even as the surgical wounds healed, the pain persisted, and Milly was in acute discomfort most of the time, so much so that the wheelchair remained in occasional use for many weeks. Walking was a struggle, and guitar

practice, which she had resumed, though for a while in a much reduced way, often had to be done half-lying on the bed. Dilation still dominated Milly's daily time-table, and the pain of it left her pale and emotionally withdrawn.

I was worried for her health in general. Milly had gone back on her hormones as soon as she got home, but something had changed and the glow that they had brought her had gone. She was frail and temperamen-tal, often feeling sick, struggling to eat and generally listless. Her hair was falling out. It was obvious to me that something more than just the process of her re-cuperation was causing problems, and I could see that Milly was not well. 'This can't be right,' I said. 'I know you're still recovering, but you should be getting better. In some ways you are, but in other ways you're worse. You need to see a doctor.'

'I can't take any more doctors,' Milly said. I could un-derstand that.

'But until you do, you won't know what's causing you to feel like this. Has anything changed in your routine?' I asked.

'Professor Frost changed my hormones before I went to Thailand,' she said. I knew that she had stopped taking the hormones before she flew because of the risk of blood clots but hadn't really thought much about what came afterwards, medically. I suppose I assumed that she was back on them now. 'He told me to go back on a half-dose after the surgery. I'm wondering if that's why I'm sick all the time and why I feel so weak.' We talked some more and I finally convinced her to see Dr Thompson again. Although I suspected this would most likely lead to another round of consultants' appointments, I was relieved when she agreed.

As I thought, Dr Thompson referred Milly straight back to Professor Frost, who, after another round of blood tests, returned her oestrogen to its original dose. She would be on this for the rest of her life. The difference was remarkable and almost immediate. Within days, Milly regained her colour and energy. She started eating and her depression lifted. And now she had her inner strength and emotional resources back, she was ready to try to find out why, after this long, she was still in chronic and extreme pain from her surgery. Milly was still bleeding and struggling to walk, yet every account she had read of sex reassignment surgery had led her to believe that at this stage, some three months after the operation, recovery would have been almost complete. In one account, Dru, the protagonist of *Becoming Drusilla* by Richard Beard, was wild camping at seven weeks after surgery. For Milly, anything approaching that level of physical exertion was inconceivable; even returning to work was out of the question.

Her first attempt at resolving the problem was to contact the Gender Identity Clinic. Although her experience of the clinic had been poor so far, she put her hope in them once again, if only for advice on her general post-operative healthcare. The hospital discharge letter from Bangkok said that she should be reviewed by a gynaecologist three months after the surgery, so, at the very least, she was expecting a referral. But the GIC waiting lists were as long as ever, and once again it was left to Dr Thompson to try to answer her plea for help. When that help finally came, in the form of an appointment with a consultant gynaecologist another three months later, her examination immediately revealed the problem. More surgery was required to remove some residual erectile tissue which was now agonisingly embedded in the reconstructed pelvic area. The natural responses of the erectile tissue were resulting in swelling and compression where there should not be any, as well as causing intermittent prolapse of the urethra. Milly's chronic pain had not been all in her mind, 'But', said the specialist as she casually signed Milly off back to the GIC, 'there's no one here who can treat you.'

Milly was desperate as the pain continued and, thanks to Dr Thompson's continuing willingness to fight for her patient, she waited yet again for another gynaecological opinion. When it came, though, the verdict was the same, though this time she was referred to a urologist. 'I don't feel safe examining you without a chaperone present,' said the gynaecologist. 'Also have you considered cognitive behavioural therapy?' But once a chaperone was duly summoned, she passed her verdict.

'Oh, hmm, you do need surgery. But I'm not trained to treat people like you. No expertise in this kind of thing. Sorry.' Although, of course, it is understandable that her consultants may have been flummoxed in the face of this unusual medical condition (lack of training in trans health issues is a serious concern in the health professions), this kind of dismissive treatment is widespread in the trans community. Many trans people report stories of their health concerns being disregarded or misinterpreted even by specialists and, equally often, of their trans status being called into the diagnosis of completely unrelated medical conditions. With sardonic bitterness, it's wryly referred to in the community as 'trans broken arm syndrome': you turn up at the emergency room with a broken bone and you're sent away with a letter to a shrink instead of a plaster cast. I was furious when Milly herself was the victim of this kind of treatment. When she was referred to an audiologist for an ear infection (a serious matter for any musician), the audiologist, seeing from her medical record that Milly was trans, dismissed her hearing test results. She needed a psychiatrist, she was told, not a hearing specialist. Even once fully transitioned, the daily battle of being trans never really comes to an end.

Throughout these months of waiting, Milly was struggling to live any kind of normal life, and I despaired as I saw her pain and watched her hope ebb away with each new appointment. Over a period of almost a year,

Milly was bounced between six different consultants at six different clinics. Every one of them agreed that she needed corrective surgery as soon as possible, and every one of them washed their hands of it. No matter how medically necessary, no one was willing to take responsibility for her care. The real tipping point, though, came with a letter from the Tavistock and Portman clinic. Milly tore it open, daring to let optimism flare briefly, though its flame was quickly extinguished: once again, her desperate physical needs were sidelined. She was offered yet another appointment with a psychiatrist. Nonetheless, when the day of the appointment arrived, Milly duly went. If she at least got through the door of the GIC, she thought, even though she was already fully transitioned, perhaps someone with real knowledge of trans health might finally offer her help.

'We don't fund corrective surgery.' The answer, when it came, was brutal. In tears, Milly begged the psychiatrist to at least let her speak to a surgeon, on the phone if nothing else. But the letter summarising their discussion which she received after the appointment made no mention of her constant struggle with bleeding, pain and despair, nor of her request to speak to a surgeon, nor of her by now well-documented need for urgent surgery. Over the next couple of months, Milly, in desperation, called the GIC many times a day to ask about the phone consultation, until eventually on her fourteenth day of calling someone picked up the phone.

The receptionist agreed to pass on her message, but after several months it was clear that the promised appointment with a surgeon was unlikely ever to materialise. Milly was angry; she seethed with fury, and now she had reached the end of the road. Utterly demoralised, she made a decision. She would go back to Thailand.

The Sarapong Clinic, on the other hand, did not find Milly's condition at all bewildering or impossible to treat. One emailed medical report later, and surgery (at no additional cost) for resection of the residual erectile tissue was booked. Nothing could be done until all the swelling around the wound sites had fully resolved and healing was complete. It was a long time to wait, and in the meantime life continued, as of course it had to. Milly was slowly getting back into a full working routine, and by the summer she was gigging again. Edwards and Dawson were often on hand to help her with the heavy gear, and I noticed a difference in how they treated her these days. Just as I had when Milly started the hormones, they now clearly perceived an essential femininity in her, and responded to her in a gentler and more protective way. Milly still held the floor when it came to the guitar, though, and any deference she received there was simply from astonishment at the freedom and virtuosity of her playing. She was, however, not infrequently disgruntled by sound engineers who, when they saw a female guitarist arrive, would set the levels to keep her sound in the background, assuming she was just there as the eye candy. Many times I had to listen to her furious dispatches from this strange new world of everyday sexism.

Although Milly was still in constant underlying pain, in every other way she was alive with happiness. Milly was confident, radiant and at ease in herself. Her international work, too, was building up again after six months off the scene, and these days she felt much more comfortable travelling alone. Her name, gender and body all matched now, and border control no longer held the same fear for her. On the other hand, going through security had become more awkward: the dilators always went in her hand luggage to avoid any possibility that they might go astray, but this meant that, as often as not, she was asked to bring them out for checking. Fortunately, she found this humorous rather than upsetting. 'It was so funny,' she recounted on one occasion, 'I had them all lined up in size order in my new velvet carrying roll, and the security lady admired them and complimented me on how well organised I kept my sex toys!' Clearly once you've put your body through everything Milly has, a public dildo inspection doesn't even register on the embarrassment scale. Other amusing moments kept her spirits up too. In Berlin, a stylist who wanted to put Milly in sexier clothes than she was comfortable with for a photo shoot told her, 'You should really experiment more with your feminine side.'

'Oh, you've got no idea how much I've done that...' Milly replied.

And back at that Berlin television station, no one questioned which changing room she should use any more or abused her in the toilets. Every new positive experience provided a counterbalance to the ever-present physical pain, and Milly never doubted for a moment that it had all been worthwhile.

During this period, I was busy too. A festival in the Netherlands came and went, another French tour, a course in Hertfordshire, with others to look forward to later in the year. Most importantly, I had sold my house. The task of downsizing, ready to start afresh, was daunting, but I worked on it single-mindedly; unwanted items went to eBay, Lucas's childhood bits and pieces to Australia, boxes to storage. Milly was finally moving into her own place, where Leigh would join her once visa issues were finalised, and I too had found a new place to call home. I don't think I had ever been so excited and optimistic as I was in preparing for these changes. After the years of unremitting stress and emotional darkness, I felt such a dawn of hope at last, and every day was full of its own small pleasures as I packed for the move and enjoyed planning for a new future. So much of the past few years had revolved around Baz's and Milly's needs, and the prospect of time and space for my own life was exhilarating. I was happy.

The months went by, consumed by the inevitable

stresses of moving house and establishing new patterns. Milly now lived nearby and would drop in often, and on these visits I soon began to notice that her anxiety was building again, as it so often had before. The thought of returning to Thailand had triggered all the traumatic memories of the previous surgery and she wasn't coping well. But there was something else brewing; I could sense it.

'I'm terrified,' she confided one afternoon, as we sat in the chilly autumn garden watching the last of the leaves glowing golden in the lowering sun. 'Terrified of the surgery. I never, ever want to go through something like that again, but because I have to, I've been thinking…'

'Yes?' I replied. Here it comes.

'I want to kill two birds with one stone. I'm thinking about having breast augmentation done at the same time. Nothing exaggerated, but I'd really love something a bit more than this A-cup. I just want a natural shape that balances the rest of my body.' The oestrogen had given Milly some curves, but it was true that she was not well-endowed.

'Will Dr Sarapong do that in the same operation?' I asked.

'Yes, I've already asked him about it,' she replied. 'I can afford it, and for me that will be it. No more surgery ever. I'll be finished.'

With that decision made, planning began in earnest. The surgery was scheduled for the following April, and once again I would go with her to Bangkok for moral support. Leigh would join us there from Connecticut and then return with Milly to England for the long term. Flights were booked, an apartment found and the costs of the surgery met. The breast augmentation was, of course, not covered by the clinic's two-for-one policy, but having the operation done at the same time as the revision surgery did mean that money was saved on the anaesthetist and the hospital bed. Costs as well as trauma were, I had to agree, considerably reduced by Milly's plan, so if this was what she wanted, it made sense. Neither of the surgeries were especially major this time, and I even hoped that I might find time to see something more of Bangkok than had been possible on the last trip. Hardly a holiday, though I could certainly do with one, but a welcome chance to recharge my batteries.

In due course, we found ourselves back in the heart of that crazy, teaming city. A different apartment this time, more conveniently located and rather less eccentric than the last. Lessons had been learnt and the public transport system was quickly mastered. I knew where the best vegan food was, where to get a decent coffee (and even an occasional glass of wine) and how much things should cost. The pre-operative consultation was on the day of our arrival, and the clinic was our first port of call. This time I also knew what to expect. It didn't make the experience any less bizarre,

but at least I wasn't surprised by the incongruous disjunct between the motorcycle parts and frying chickens
and glamorous young women carrying their little bags
tied with ribbons. Dr Sarapong's waiting times hadn't
improved, and I was sufficiently confident in his poor
timekeeping that I could take the opportunity to have
a massage above the motorcycle repair shop for a few
hundred baht and emerge feeling more relaxed than I
had in months. There was even time for something to
eat at the excellent street restaurant a few doors along.
These days, I was quite a Bangkok *habituée*.

The surgery was the day after we arrived, and we were
taken by chauffeur from our apartment to the Samitivej Hospital in Chinatown. A mere hour and half in
the car on this occasion, though I quickly discovered I
could walk it in fifteen minutes. Milly was nervous and
reluctant for either Leigh or me to leave her side while
she was prepared for surgery, and the day passed slowly
as we waited for her to be taken to theatre. For me, the
tension was unbearable. I find hospitals extremely confronting, perhaps from too many upsetting experiences,
but I had to admit the Samitivej was the height of
professionalism and luxury. When it was time, I kissed
Milly on the cheek and squeezed her hand. 'It'll be fine,'
I said, because that's what mothers say.

For the next two hours I simply meandered, absorb-
ing the sights and sounds and smells all around me. I
distracted myself with a visit to Wat Traimit, the temple

of the Golden Buddha, conveniently situated next to the hospital, and wondered how many people went there to offer up a prayer while they waited for news of their loved ones over the road. Evening had fallen and Chinatown had taken on a new life in the time that I had been wandering its streets. It was now crowded with people in pursuit of their next meal, and row after row of roast ducks hung suspended on hooks in steamy glass cabinets, tempting the passers-by. The La Scala shark fin restaurant was doing a roaring trade too, but caught my attention mainly for its incongruous operatic name; I'd been working a lot on Italian opera scores recently, but here in Bangkok I would leave its shark fins to the enthusiasts. And then at last I got the call from Leigh telling me that Milly was back in her room. Awake, fine. And she was.

Leigh stayed overnight, and when I arrived back the next morning Milly was sitting up in bed. Her upper body was swathed in bandages and a drain led out from underneath them to a bag on the bedside, which was filling with pale red fluid. She was smiling with delight. It was strange to see her propped up against the pillows with her bandaged chest tenderly covered with a sheet, and a palpable sense of lightness emanated from her. But there was another, more serious note. 'I don't hurt any more,' Milly said in quiet wonder. 'I mean, yes, it hurts because of the surgery. But the pain, all that deep pain that never stopped, has totally gone.' She was

overcome by a sense of release from the physical suffering that had shadowed her every step for the past year,
and tears of relief and joy ran down her cheeks. It was
an emotional moment for all of us.

Milly was discharged from hospital a couple of days
later and spent the next week resting. Already she
was walking easily, but the revision surgery and new
stitches had made dilation very painful once again. The
procedure was draining for her and, coupled with not
being able to shower for the time being, her inclination
was simply to cocoon herself in the air-conditioned
comfort of the apartment. I, on the other hand, was
now at large in the city, relishing the opportunity to
wander without map or purpose. This time, Bangkok
was fun. I walked for miles, rode in tuk-tuks and took
boats down back-street canals, visiting temples and
monasteries and markets. It was now mid-April and
everywhere the streets were lined with stalls selling
golden flowers. Street corner Buddhas were garlanded
with marigolds, and in the lobby of our apartment
building and even at the Sarapong Clinic, when Milly
went for a post-operative check-up, small shrines had
appeared, dressed with statues of the Buddha and bowls
of water surrounded by foliage and flowers. A video
started to play on a loop in the apartment lift, and
although it was incomprehensible to me, being in Thai,
it seemed to involve cartoon people of all ages being

sternly warned against irresponsible water throwing. '*Suk san wan Songkran*,' they shouted, upending buckets over hapless scooter riders; X went the bold red graphic across the screen. Something was clearly happening in Bangkok, but as I was neither tourist nor local, I had no idea what that might be.

I soon got the memo, though. *Songkran* is the great Buddhist water festival that celebrates Thai New Year. By the sheerest chance we were here at the time of this colourful holiday, and Bangkok, lively at any time, was now ratcheting up the excitement. Music and light shows pulsated through the night, and every day heaps of gold and white flowers appeared on the street, along with hawkers selling plastic capes and waterproof satchels for mobile phones. Every shop was doing a roaring side business in Super Soakers and high-pressure water pistols, and clothing stalls had replaced their usual workaday stock with vibrantly coloured T-shirts and dresses covered in flower prints. There was no avoiding the spirit of *Songkran* in Bangkok, and the enthusiasm was infectious. Milly was now well on the road to recovery and we had taken a few trips to the shopping mall and out to eat, but she was still very much convalescing and took her post-operative care extremely seriously. She would do nothing that might undo the healing process that had finally brought her to this place of deliriously happy relief. I, on the other hand, was more than ready for fun, and the bright colours and joyous cavalcade of noise in the streets below our apartment were calling me.

I ventured out into the humid afternoon and headed for the MRT, the Bangkok underground train system. Guards were on water pistol duty, and no one was allowed into the station ticket hall until their gun was proved empty. In my brightly coloured sundress, I melted into the crowd and was pulled along by its energy. Silom, I punched into the ticket machine. Seven baht. If I'd thought I might have a quiet stroll, entertained by some gentle water fun, I was much mistaken. Today was New Year's Day itself in Thailand, the climax of the holiday, and all Bangkok was at Silom Station, spilling out in their thousands and tens of thousands onto Silom and Narathiwat Roads. The streets were a blaze of noise and colour, with food stalls smoking deliciously in side alleys and the more enterprising entrepreneurs selling not water pistols but the water to top them up with. Five baht per fill. It was chaos.

My spirits were light. Milly had come through her final surgery. She was well again, safe, happy. After a lifetime's journey to find herself, Milly had arrived, bringing me along with her. I had learnt so much, seen so much pain, despaired at so much suffering and been grateful for so much kindness. There was, she told me, never a moment of regret, no matter how gruelling the road had been at times. At last, she looked forward to her future, able to envisage a life for herself, full of optimism for whatever prospects might lie ahead. Here on Silom Road, we were all, in one way or another, celebrating new beginnings.

'Look out!' someone shouted, as a gaggle of teenage boys turned their *Songkran* Super Soakers on me. They laughed uproariously as they took aim and, too slow, I was drenched from head to toe. I ran to the low wall at the edge of the station stairs, and as I sat there in the water-laden heat of the afternoon, all my thoughts were of the three of us – Milly, Leigh and me – here in this strange city. Dripping wet, surrounded by colour and hope, I laughed and cried and laughed as though I would never stop. Happy New Year, Milly.

EPILOGUE

Two roads diverged in a yellow wood,
And sorry I could not travel both
And be one traveler, long I stood
And looked down one as far as I could
To where it bent in the undergrowth;

Then took the other, as just as fair,
And having perhaps the better claim,
Because it was grassy and wanted wear;
Though as for that the passing there
Had worn them really about the same,

And both that morning equally lay
In leaves no step had trodden black.
Oh, I kept the first for another day!
Yet knowing how way leads on to way,
I doubted if I should ever come back.

I shall be telling this with a sigh
Somewhere ages and ages hence:
Two roads diverged in a wood and I –
I took the one less traveled by,
And that has made all the difference.

– 'The Road Not Taken' by Robert Frost (1874–1963)

At the end of the road, all travellers tell their tales. The old recount their glory days, the adventurers the strange and wonderful places they have seen. The Viking sagas and the histories of Magellan and Columbus speak to us of the seductive call of the unknown. There are stories, like Darwin's *Voyage of the Beagle*, that change our world for ever; and others, like those in Hakluyt's *Principal Navigations*, that sometimes owe as much to the realm of the imagination as they do to documentary. But every tale of every path, no matter how humble, contains in it the power to captivate and teach us. This is the way of the traveller. In the end, every life is its own journey, and by embracing it we learn who we really are. On that journey, if we are living well, we choose the roads that we will travel, and we embrace the consequences of those choices. Or we can just let life happen to us, and in that there will also be a story, though we will not be its author. Choosing the road less travelled always requires courage, and being the author of your life means taking responsibility for your footsteps along that way. It also means understanding and accepting that change is growth. When we fear change and try to hide or protect ourselves from it, we also close our lives to the gifts that it brings.

Just five years ago, I knew nothing of the inner world of my daughter. I did not know my own child. I knew nothing of the sorrow and suffering of transgender people, of their history and experience, of their fears and their courage. I did not know that my journey would take me to places every bit as foreign as Marco Polo's silk road or Leif Erikson's Vinland, and if I had thought about it, I doubt I could ever have foreseen the point that I have finally arrived at. I have lived through the extraordinary experience of seeing my child born a second time in a new body, and in that process I have had to face shortcomings of my own. There have been many mistakes, and times when I have hurt my daughter with thoughtless comments. I regret them, but more often than not they have come from ignorance, and in them have been the seeds of my own growth. But the important point is, I suppose, that I have been willing to learn, and I have tried to find in myself the courage to embrace change. And in doing so, my life has been immeasurably enriched.

All enduring stories have, I think, a mythic element, by which I do not mean that they are made up but that they hold in them some deeper truths that resonate across time. Such tales are the threads that connect us with ourselves; those journeys scribe their paths across the map of our heart. For me, the mythos of the story of my daughter's transition is that our experiences form an arc through life: we are spirit, flesh, bones and, in the end (I like to think), spirit again. My child came to me, female in spirit, drawn perhaps by my own inner conviction of my baby's gender. But her body was, in all its outward appearance, male, and for twenty-two long and difficult years she was hidden in that flesh, concealing her spirit from the world. There are those who will only accept as real that which is manifest physically, and even among my own family there is loss because of this. I grieve for the unreconciled differences between my children, for future nieces and nephews who may never know their aunt, for my own brother and sister who may always be divided by their views.

But flesh is mutable and today, through the great and generous skill of endocrinologists and surgeons, spirit can be reincarnated in the physical form for which it yearns. Metamorphosis has always been a theme that speaks to us in stories, not least because it carries within it the truth that we all have the capacity to transform ourselves or to be transformed, whether by will or by circumstance. The prospect of transformation is one that gives all of us hope, in one way or another.

What really matters is not what is written by our chromosomes in the bone but what is written by our lives. The expression of our spirit and our creativity, our capacity to grow and change, the way we

embrace our search for love and seize on its precious-
ness when we find it. Our life's legacy lies in how we
have lived it, not in what any physical remains may tell.
The road to my daughter has led me deep into knowing
who I am and what I want to be in this world. I took the
road less travelled by, and that made all the difference.

ACKNOWLEDGEMENTS

My thanks and great appreciation to the team at Biteback Publishing for their confidence in this book, their unfailing support, and their tolerance of slipped deadlines when life intervened. Early in this journey I was told by a wise and experienced writer that the most important thing was that my book find the right editor, someone who would fight to bring it into the world. I am very grateful to Olivia Beattie for being that person.

My deepest appreciation also to my agent, Caroline Hardman of Hardman and Swainson. Without her support and vision, this book would not have found its home.

I am also immensely grateful to Clare Lynch, who is really the godmother of this book. Clare encouraged me to tell my story and was passionate about its worth. Her guidance through the writing process was invaluable.

Most of all, of course, I am deeply grateful to my daughter, without whom this book would not have been written. She read drafts and shared her insights, thoughts and experiences with great dignity and generosity. I am honoured to have her in my life.

ENDNOTES

CHAPTER 1

Morris, Jan, *Conundrum*, Faber & Faber, 1974. The iconic memoir of a pioneering transition.

CHAPTER 2

On deadnaming
Clements, K. C., 'What Is Deadnaming?', Healthline, 2018, https://www.healthline.com/health/transgender/deadnaming

CHAPTER 3

On trans suicide risk
Bradlow, J., Bartram, F., Guasp, A. and Jadva, V., 'School Report: The experiences of lesbian, gay, bi and trans

young people in Britain's schools in 2017', Stonewall, 2017, pp. 30–31, https://www.stonewall.org.uk/system/files/the_school_report_2017.pdf

Herman, J., Brown, T. and Haas, A., 'Suicide Thoughts and Attempts Among Transgender Adults: Findings from the 2015 U.S. Transgender Survey', Williams Institute, UCLA School of Law, 2019, https://williamsinstitute.law.ucla.edu/publications/suicidality-transgender-adults/

McNeil, J., Bailey, L., Ellis, S., Morton, J. and Regan, M., 'Trans Mental Health Study 2012', Scottish Transgender Alliance, 2012, p. 59, https://www.gires.org.uk/wp-content/uploads/2014/08/trans_mh_study.pdf

On anorexia among trans teenagers
Diemer, E., Grant, J., Munn-Chernoff, M., Patterson, D. and Duncan, A., 'Gender Identity, Sexual Orientation, and Eating-Related Pathology in a National Sample of College Students', *Journal of Adolescent Health*, 57/2, 2015, pp. 144–9, https://www.jahonline.org/article/S1054-139X(15)00087-7/fulltext

Guss, C., Williams, D., Reisner, S., Austin, S. B. and Katz-Wise, S., 'Disordered Weight Management Behaviors, Nonprescription Steroid Use, and Weight Perception in Transgender Youth', *Journal of Adolescent*

Health, 60/1, 2016, pp. 17–22, https://www.jahonline.org/
article/S1054-139X(16)30321-4/fulltext

Harvey, R., 'Eating Disorders Do Not Discriminate: Trans
Teens Face Greater Risk', Penn Medicine News, 2019,
https://www.pennmedicine.org/news/news-blog/2019/
march/eating-disorders-do-not-discriminate-trans-
teens-face-greater-risk

CHAPTER 4

On Tara Hudson and the Ministry of Justice
Townsend, M., 'Transgender woman sues over
ordeal in male prison', *The Guardian*, 20 January 2018,
https://www.theguardian.com/society/2018/jan/20/
tara-hudson-transgender-prisoner-sues-government

CHAPTER 5

On the 'third gender'
'Legal recognition of non-binary gender', Wikipedia,
https://en.wikipedia.org/wiki/Legal_recognition_of_
non-binary_gender. A useful summary with further
reading.

On the concept and history of 'two spirit'
Ebert, T. and Whitcomb, P., 'Origin of the Term "Two
Spirit"', Natural Resources Conservation Service, http://

www.nrcs.usda.gov/wps/PA_NRCSConsumption/
download?cid=nrcseprd1166407&ext=pdf

Neptune, G., 'What Does Two-Spirit Mean?', Inqueery,
Season 1, Ep. 11, *Them*, 2018, https://www.them.us/
video/watch/geo-neptune-explains-two-spirit

On transgender in history
Laqueur, T., *Making Sex: Body and Gender from the
Greeks to Freud*, Harvard University Press, 1990.

CHAPTER 7

On discrimination in employment
'Transphobia rife among UK employers as 1 in 3 won't hire
a transgender person', Crossland Employment Solicitors,
2018, https://www.crosslandsolicitors.com/site/hr-hub/
transgender-discrimination-in-UK-workplaces

CHAPTER 8

On family and social rejection
Grant, J. et al., 'Injustice at Every Turn: A Report of
the National Transgender Discrimination Survey',
National Center for Transgender Equality, 2011, https://
transequality.org/sites/default/files/docs/resources/
NTDS_Report.pdf

CHAPTER 9

On voice therapy: a brief overview
'Voice feminizing therapy and surgery', Mayo Clinic, 2019, https://www.mayoclinic.org/tests-procedures/voice-feminizing-therapy-and-surgery/about/pac-20470545

CHAPTER 13

On treatment waiting times
'The Waiting List for NHS Gender Identity Clinics: Patients' Experiences', GenderGP, 18 February 2020, https://www.gendergp.com/the-waiting-list-for-nhs-gender-identity-clinic-gic-patients-experiences/

Parsons, V., 'Trans patients are being forced to wait up to 193 weeks for vital healthcare. The NHS target is 18 weeks', PinkNews, 13 August 2020, https://www.pinknews.co.uk/2020/08/13/nhs-trans-patients-laurels-gender-identity-clinic-south-west-waiting-list-yeovil-pride/

On the mental health impact of hormone therapy
McNeil, J., Bailey, L., Ellis, S., Morton, J. and Regan, M., 'Trans Mental Health Study 2012', Scottish Transgender Alliance, 2012, pp. 20–21, https://www.gires.org.uk/wpcontent/uploads/2014/08/trans_mh_study.pdf

On self-prescribing hormones
Metastasio, A., Martinotti, G., Corazza, O. and Negri, A., 'Transitioning Bodies. The Case of Self-Prescribing Sexual Hormones in Gender Affirmation in Individuals Attending Psychiatric Services', *Brain Sciences*, 8/5, May 2018, p. 88, https://www.researchgate.net/publication/325129937_Transitioning_Bodies_The_Case_of_Self-Prescribing_Sexual_Hormones_in_Gender_Affirmation_in_Individuals_Attending_Psychiatric_Services

On the effect of anti-androgens on aggressive behaviour
Cunningham, R., Lumia, A. and McGinnis, M., 'Androgen Receptors, Sex Behaviour, and Aggression', *Neuroendocrinology*, 96/2, 2012, pp. 131–40, https://www.ncbi.nlm.nih.gov/pmc/articles/PMC3474193/

CHAPTER 16

On current medical science
Garcia-Falgueras, A. and Swaab, D., 'Sexual hormones and the brain: an essential alliance for sexual identity and sexual orientation', *Endocrine Development*, 17, 2010, pp. 22–35.

Kranz, G. et al., 'White Matter Microstructure in Transsexuals and Controls Investigated by Diffusion

Tensor Imaging', *The Journal of Neuroscience*, 34/46, 2014, pp. 15466–15475.

Sapolsky, R., 'Caught Between Male and Female', *Wall Street Journal*, 6 December 2013, https://www.wsj.com/articles/SB10001424052702304854804579234030532617704

Williams, S., 'Are the Brains of Transgender People Different from those of Cisgender People?', *The Scientist*, 1 March 2018, https://www.the-scientist.com/features/are-the-brains-of-transgender-people-different-from-those-of-cisgender-people-30027

World Health Organization, 'WHO/Europe brief – transgender health in the context of ICD-11', 2020, https://www.euro.who.int/en/health-topics/health-determinants/gender/gender-definitions/whoeurope-brief-transgender-health-in-the-context-of-icd-11

CHAPTER 19

On discrimination in trans healthcare

Robinson, F., 'Caring for LGBT patients in the NHS', *British Medical Journal*, 366/l5374, 2019.

Whitehead, B., 'Inequalities in Access to Healthcare for Transgender Patients', *Links to Health and Social Care*, 2/1, 2017, pp. 63–7.

A BRIEF GUIDE TO FURTHER READING

Baker, Sarah, *Transgender Behind Prison Walls*, Water-side, 2017

Boylan, Jennifer, *She's Not There: A Life in Two Genders*, Broadway, 2004

Burns, Christine (ed.), *Trans Britain: Our Journey from the Shadows*, Unbound, 2018

Cossey, Caroline, *My Story*, Faber & Faber, 1992

Craggs, Charlie, *To My Trans Sisters*, Jessica Kingsley, 2017

Dawson, Juno, *The Gender Games: The Problem with Men and Women, From Someone Who Has Been Both*, Two Roads, 2018

Erickson-Schroth, Laura and Jacobs, Laura, *You're in The Wrong Bathroom: And 20 Other Myths and Misconceptions About Transgender and Gender-Nonconforming People*, Beacon, 2017

Fine, Cordelia, *Testosterone Rex: Myths of Sex, Science and Society*, Icon Books, 2018

Henry, Declan, *Trans Voices: Becoming Who You Are*, Jessica Kingsley, 2017

Jacques, Juliet, *Trans: A Memoir*, Verso, 2015

Jeffreys, Sheila, *Gender Hurts: A Feminist Analysis of the Politics of Transgenderism*, Routledge, 2013

Lester, C. N., *Trans Like Me: A Journey for All of Us*, Virago, 2017

Mock, Janet, *Redefining Realness: My Path to Womanhood, Identity, Love and So Much More*, Atria, 2014

Morris, Jan, *Conundrum*, Faber & Faber, 1974

Paige, Caroline, *True Colours: My Life as the First Openly Transgender Officer in the British Armed Forces*, Biteback, 2017

Stryker, Susan, *Transgender History: The Roots of Today's Revolution*, 2nd ed., Seal, 2017

Styles, Rhyannon, *The New Girl*, Headline, 2017